San Francisco Chinatown

A Walking Tour

by Shirley Fong-Torres

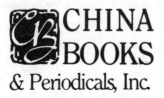

CHINA BOOKS & Periodicals, Inc.

Photo credits: pp. *xxiv*, 46, 48, 53, 54, 56, 116 — San Francisco
Convention and Visitors Bureau; pp. 10, 23, 26, 27, 52, 140 —
Bancroft Library, University of California; p. 12 — courtesy of Larry
Mak; p. 13 — courtesy of the author's parents, Connie and Richard
Fong-Torres; pp. 21, 23, 86, 87, 89, 90, 97, 98, 107, 108, 109, 111,
112, 118, 122, 123, 124, 126, 135, 144 — Nancy Ippolito; pp. *xiv*, 24,
25, 33, 34, 44, 68, 73, 78, 80, 82, 115, 140 — Frank Cimo; p. 36 —
Y.K.M. Studio; p. 36 — Russell Jong; pp.104, 178 — Sharon Beals

Cover design by Rick Wong
Text design by Linda Revel
Cover photographs by Sharon Beals
Calligraphy by Y. K. Lau

Library of Congress Catalog Card Number: 91-72060

ISBN 0-8351-2436-3

Printed in the United States of America by   CHINA
BOOKS
& Periodicals, Inc.

DEDICATION

To my daughter, Kristina Carrie Dong

&

in loving memory of my brother, Barry,
a community worker in
San Francisco's Chinatown

Contents

ACKNOWLEDGMENTS

Many of my friends, family members, and colleagues contributed their time, effort, and knowledge to assist me in writing this book. I greatly appreciate their friendship.

I wish to thank my editor, Bob Schildgen, and Nancy Ippolito, head of the books division at China Books, for believing in me, and for their guidance. I salute my staff: Madeline Sherry, who keeps me organized; Wok Wiz tour leaders Ophelia Wong, Larry Mak, George Mew, Rhoda Wing, Hank Quock, Martha Mew, Dorothy Quock, and Bernice Fong—bright and witty Chinatown experts, each of whom I am very proud; Martin Yan, my dear friend and colleague to whom I often turn for advice, and with whom I share the joy of wokking and walking with others; Linda Revel, gifted graphic designer; Sharon Beals, Frank Cimo, and Nancy Ippolito, ace photographers; Y. K. and Gary Lau, for art and calligraphy in this book; the staff of the Huntington Hotel; the management and staff of Holiday Inn, Chinatown, and especially General Manager George de Battha and Sales Manager Gerlinde Simone; Ethel Watkins for assistance at the San Francisco Public Library in digging up research materials; Monica Rosenthal of the Buena Vista Winery; historian William Heintz and journalist Gaye Le Baron; San Francisco Convention & Visitors Bureau; Angel Island Association; Chinese Historical Society Museum and Chinese Cultural Center; U.C. Berkeley

Bancroft Library; Lincoln Lim of Mow Fung Produce; the Lew family of Feng Haung Pastry; Ten Ren Tea Shop and Silver Restaurant; Cliff Chow of Harbor Village Restaurant; Frank and Nancy at the Golden Gate Fortune Cookie Factory; Lulu Leon and Michael Lau and their lively kung fu students; the San Francisco Police Department's magnificent lion dance team; my good friend Mark Gordon of Frisco Tours; my fun-loving cooking students from points all over the world; my sweet daughter Kristina Dong for helping in the office and kitchen; Angie and Ray Campodonico; Joyce and Brian Narlock; Rose and Bernard Carver for tasting new recipes; to my mother and father for making the journey to America; to my brother Ben, of whom I am always proud; to my dear and loving husband Bernie Carver, who has been with me every step of the way throughout the hundreds of hours it took to complete this book. Last but not least, I thank the thousands of friends whom I have met on our Chinatown walks and through our cooking programs.

Shirley Fong-Torres

FOREWORD

I have known Shirley for a number of years and am always impressed with her knowledge of San Francisco's Chinatown. Now she has combined the many facets of Chinatown in this new volume: the history, culture, and cuisine of the residents living and working there. She brings interest by infusing historical notes and rich insights into Chinatown's cultural heritage. This book is an invaluable companion for self-guided tours or for armchair visitors who want to know more about this world-famous location. I have been visiting and working in San Francisco's Chinatown for many years, and still find it intriguing and exciting.

Shirley is a true professional. Besides her knowledge and enthusiasm, she knows the restaurant business, especially Chinese cuisine, from the ground up. She grew up in her father's restaurant and helped as soon as she began walking. She is still wokking, but harder. Her insightful details on Chinese produce and shopping tips were part of a recent segment on my *Yan Can Cook* show.

Shirley has seemingly unlimited enthusiasm and energy in sharing her understanding of Chinatown with the public. Many know her through her cable television cooking program, cooking classes, Chinatown tours, articles about Chinese food and restaurants, and her first book, *Wok Wiz Chinatown Tour Cookbook.*

It is with great pleasure that I introduce *San Francisco Chinatown: A Walking Tour* as fascinating and thoroughly educational. It is a timely expression of a talented, resourceful, and knowledgeable professional, and most certainly a valuable and enjoyable resource for anyone interested in Chinatown.

—Martin Yan, *Yan Can Cook* **Television Series**

INTRODUCTION

The Chinese-Americans in San Francisco have a short but exciting history. Our forefathers burst on the scene during the gold rush era in the late 1840s, and led the way to enable us to become respected citizens one and a half centuries later. It is through their inner strength, willingness to work, endurance of mental and physical abuse and racial prejudice that our greater strengths fused together. The Chinese-Americans are a powerful force in this country today.

Our Chinatown community is one of the top attractions for locals and visitors to our beautiful city. Over 30,000 Asians live in this 24-square-block area, and as the numbers increase, movement to other neighborhoods in San Francisco is apparent. A "New Chinatown" thrives in the Richmond district of our city.

I am proud to share Chinatown and its people through our walking tour programs. As the years progressed, my goal for our tours became clearer: to promote cultural understanding of the people of San Francisco's Chinatown. We hire tour leaders who are very personable, knowledgeable, and enthusiastic about Chinatown. Wok Wiz tour leaders represent ages from 30-something to 70-something, so each person brings a different perspective to the tour based on his or her background. Several of our Wok Wiz tour leaders were born and raised in Chinatown, and many are Chinese-food experts or teachers.

In 1987, I was the Wok Wiz Chinatown Tour Company, running the business by myself. Today, with the help of my staff, we sometimes host over 100 visitors a day on morning or evening tours. In 1990, we introduced a subsidiary called A Taste of Chinatown! which operates under the Gray Line Tours umbrella. Known as Tour #9, A Taste of Chinatown! is a walking tour that focuses on the architecture and history of the area. Our next venture is to conduct Angel Island tours.

I hope that readers of this book will gain a better understanding of this magnificent city within a city, alleys

Wok Wiz Team: (left to right): Hank Quock, Rhoda Wing, Larry Mak, Shirley Fong-Torres, Ophelia Wong, Bernie Carver, George Mew. Not pictured: Martha Mew, Bernice Fong, and Dorothy Quock.

within alleys, and the people who live and work here. Years ago, other tour companies dwelt on our "wicked" past in order to sensationalize this neighborhood. The Chinese have their vices, just as most other people do, but they are more of a footnote than the real story. My forefathers played major roles in contributing to the economic and social development of San Francisco and the country.

Over the years, we have met individuals, families, honeymooners, newcomer and senior citizens clubs, and church and school groups. We organize special walks and cooking events for many of our corporate accounts and spousal programs. Some of the absolutely funniest and most memorable groups include: "Winos on Wheels," a group of bicycling buddies from Marin County across the Golden Gate Bridge; "Stitches 'n Bitches," seamstresses from the Gold Country; the "Rotterdam Rowdies," who flew from Victoria, B.C., and came directly to the tour from the airport, and left promptly afterward to shop until they dropped at the San Francisco Center; the "W.O.W." group of widows and widowers; the "Big Benders," my own close friends who tricked me by signing up for the tour under a false group name; five women who drove almost six hours from Lake Tahoe in the nick of time for the tour; and Carl Dunn's church group who took a leisurely two-hour train ride from San Jose, California. The most misunderstood group that I booked was the "Anti-Aging Group." I was quite puzzled and questioned why they would want to go on my tour if they were "Anti-Asian." Fortunately, they were quick to correct my faulty hearing.

People have surprised loved ones by flying them into San Francisco to sign up for our tours for Valentine's Day, birthdays, or anniversaries. Every day is special for my Wok Wiz tour leaders and me, as we never know who we will meet.

It is with much love and affection that I present this book, with the hope that you will enjoy reading about Chinatown, and will whip up a few dishes in your wok using the easy recipes in the back of the book.

How to Use this Book

This book is designed to help you join me on a historical, cultural, and culinary tour of San Francisco's Chinatown. You can make this tour in several different ways. Read through and make an armchair trip. Browse for general information in planning your own visit to Chinatown. Select some of the many places discussed and spend some time at each one. Or, if you want the full treatment, and you like to walk, you can follow the tour exactly, and visit every single one of the more than 50 locations noted here! Nothing quite compares to experiencing Chinatown on foot—whether you amble through two blocks or wander the whole route of a little over a mile. It can take a few hours or more than a day, depending on your mood, your energy level, and your inclination to shop! We recommend starting off fairly early in the morning and then sitting down to enjoy a *dim sum* luncheon some time before one o'clock in the afternoon (see Chapter 13). The entire walk itself should not be difficult for anyone in good physical condition. Dress casually and wear good walking shoes. With the exception of two optional detours, the route described here avoids the steepest part of Chinatown in the mostly residential area above Stockton Street. But however you go, enjoy. Whether I conduct tours in person or through these pages, my goal is always to help visitors make the most of their journey to this enticing community.

The **MAP** immediately following serves as a general guide, and we proceed chapter by chapter to the various locations, each of which is listed in **boldface** for convenience.

The section right after the map tells you **How to Get to Chinatown,** if you are unfamiliar with the transportation systems.

I've tried to make the discussions casual and comfortable, to sound just as if we were walking along together on a tour. On several occasions, I revert to my former role as a teacher, presenting historical and cultural information that is not generally known outside of the Chinese community. You will take peeks into the past as well as learn about the present. At the same time, there are many sprinkles of personal observations, anecdotes, and comments about experiences of my Wok Wiz tour leaders.

The book is divided into two sections: the first part presents the various locations on the tour, giving a little background about each; the second part is a culinary guide and cookbook which includes 42 of my favorite recipes. Trying some of the recipes may set the mood for your visit, or bring back memories after you've gone home. Since Chinese food is best when shared with friends, most of the recipes are grouped as complete meals or as menus for special parties. The recipes reflect my preference for healthful, nutritious meals quickly and simply prepared. For those who wish to dine in Chinatown, there is also a list of my favorite Chinese restaurants.

Recommended

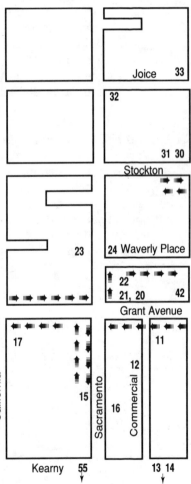

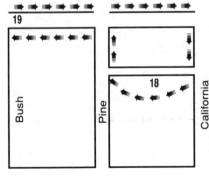

Attractions in CHINATOWN:

41. I-Chong Art Gallery, 661 Jackson Street
42. Kee Fung Ng Gallery, 757 Grant
43. Fat Ming Co., 903 Grant
44. Chew Chong Tai & Co., 905 Grant
45. Ping Yuen Bakery, 650 Jackson
46. Ginn Wall Hardware, 1016 Grant
47. Kwong Jow Sausage, 1157 Grant
48. Metro Food Company, 641 Broadway
49. May Wah Co., 1230 Stockton

50. Wo Soon Produce, 1210 Stockton
51. Wing Sun Market, 1135 Stockton
52. Feng Huang Pastry Shop, 761 Jackson
53. ✻ Chinese Cultural Center, 750 Kearny St.
54. ✻ East Wind Book Store, 633 Vallejo St.
55. ✻ Wells Fargo History Room,
    420 Montgomery
56. ✻ Cable Car Barn & Museum, 1201 Mason

✻ Indicates site is located off of map

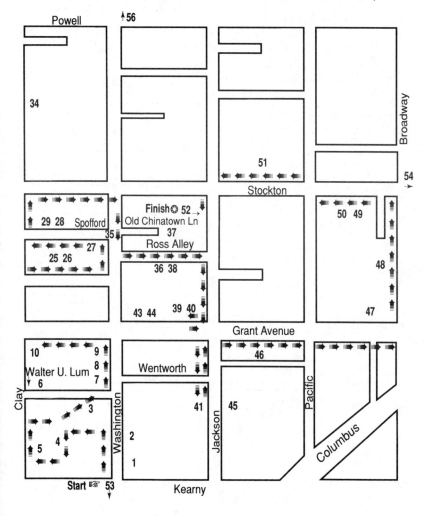

How to Get to Chinatown

San Francisco is a very compact city with good public transportation. Our compactness often leads to traffic congestion and parking difficulties. This is especially true in Chinatown. Although it is enjoyable to visit any time of the day, Chinatown is much less congested in the mornings, and that is when we start most of our tours.

Walking from Hotels

Many of the guests on our tours walk from the major hotels in the city. Union Square is just eight blocks from Portsmouth Square, where we begin. To walk from Union Square, go east to Kearny Street, and turn left on Kearny. Follow Kearny to Portsmouth Square. This walk is level or downhill.

Most of the hotels near Fisherman's Wharf are about 12 blocks away from Portsmouth Square. If you follow Columbus Street, the walk will be only slightly uphill. You know you're in Chinatown when you see the business signs in Chinese.

Mass Transit

An excellent way to get to Chinatown from many points in the Bay Area is on BART, the Bay Area Rapid Transit system. If you have a car, you can drive to the nearest BART station, park there for free, and avoid the stress of traffic. Many local bus systems feed into BART. For information on BART and related systems call (415) 788-BART.

The BART stop closest to Portsmouth Square is the Montgomery Street station. From this station walk one block west to Kearny Street, make a right turn and walk six blocks or take the #15 bus. The #15, 30, and 41 bus lines all pass through Chinatown. The 15 also connects to the Caltrain system from the South Bay and the Peninsula. From other bus transit systems which come into the Transbay Terminal walk west on Mission Street to Third Street for the #15 bus. For specific advice on bus transportation, call (415) 673-MUNI.

Driving

If you decide to drive, parking is most reasonable and usually available at one of the municipal garages, like Portsmouth Square at Clay and Kearny Streets, or the one at the corner of Sutter and Stockton Streets.

San Francisco has graphic signs directing tourists to Chinatown, but the following directions will give you a head start:

From the North

If you are driving from the north, follow Highway 101 toward "downtown" to Lombard Street and then to Van Ness Avenue. Make a left turn from Van Ness onto Bush Street, which will take you to Chinatown. Make a left turn on Kearny to get to Portsmouth Square.

From the South

If you are driving from the south, take Highway 101 to Highway 80 and toward the Bay Bridge. Exit from Highway 80 at the Fourth Street off ramp, which is the last San Francisco exit before the bridge. From this exit, continue east on Bryant Street for one block. Make a left turn from Bryant to Third Street. Follow Third Street to Market Street and cross Market. On the other side of Market, Third Street becomes Kearny Street, which will lead you directly to Chinatown and Portsmouth Square.

From the East

If you are driving from the East Bay on the Bay Bridge, get in the right lane when you approach San Francisco. Take the Fremont Street exit, and follow Fremont to Market Street. Make a left turn onto Market Street, and follow Market to Kearny Street. Make a right turn on Kearny and follow it to Chinatown.

The Cable Cars

Probably the most fun way to get to Chinatown is on one of the cable cars for which San Francisco is famous (and which are considered a must-ride for all visitors). Any of the three cable car lines will take you to Chinatown. The fare is $2.00 for adults as of this writing. If you want to save money on transportation, get a one- or three- day "MUNI passport," which can be used on the cable cars as well as the buses. Call the number above for information.

CHAPTER 1

A visit to any location is always more fascinating if you know something of its history, and this is as true of Chinatown as any other place.

THE CHINESE IN AMERICA: A HISTORICAL PRELUDE

To understand why Chinatown exists today, it is important to know some of its history. To many people, Chinatown has always been a mysterious place, and its origins remain obscure even to those who live there.

It is possible that some ancient Chinese actually set foot on the American continent over a thousand years before Chinatown began, long before the Europeans arrived. There are references in Chinese literature from the fifth century A.D. to a land called *Fusang*, located seven thousand miles east of Japan. A Buddhist missionary named Hui Shan was said to have reported to the emperor's court in 499 that he visited this land. *Fusang* was the name of a magical tree that grew in the new land, with leaves that resembled bamboo when they first came out. The natives were said to consume its pear-like fruit, use its fiber for clothing, and write on its bark. Proponents of the fusang theory claim that the maguey tree, which played an important part in Aztec civilization, fits this description. They also point to a number of other lines of the ancient text which appear to describe customs and geographical features unique to the American continent. The use of jade is a prime example of the similarities in the two cultures. Both the Chinese and Mexicans felt that jade had magical powers that made it the most precious of all the earth's resources. Both placed funeral jades painted with red cinnabar in the mouths of their dead.

Seasoned navigators of the Pacific have verified that prevailing ocean currents in the Pacific could have helped Chinese mariners reach North America. At this point in history Chinese sailors had a sailing technology, including the compass, and boats that could have made it possible to voyage as far as America.

There is another ancient manuscript which claims that a mariner named Hee-li arrived on a distant shore after a long voyage caused by a storm and a defective compass. Its description of the shoreline does sound very much like the area around Monterey and San Francisco. Archeological evidence of Chinese visits includes stone anchors recently discovered near the California coast which are like those used by ancient Chinese sailors.

THE FIRST CHINESE TRAVELERS TO SAN FRANCISCO

Unsubstantiated stories abound regarding the first Chinese arrivals in San Francisco. One story concerned a Chinese cabin boy on board the ship *Bolivar* that sailed into San Francisco Bay in 1838. After a brief stay, he left on the ship loaded with its cargo of tallow and hides. Another version claims that a young Cantonese merchant, Chung Ming, arrived in 1847 and returned to China to spread the news among his countrymen about the gold in California. A third variation suggests that two men and a woman arrived on the ship *Eagle* on February 2, 1848. Each of the three stories lacks documentary proof because of six fires in the city between 1849 and 1851 which destroyed many historical documents. We are certain, however, that there were Chinese here by the time the Gold Rush started when James Marshall discovered gold in the California foothills east of San Francisco. A surviving editorial from the San Francisco *Star* of April 1, 1848 mentions the presence of two or three Chinese who had found ready employment.

Like adventurous young men throughout the world, many Chinese came to California with the hope of finding riches in our Gold Country. California soon became known in China as *Gum San*, meaning "Gold Mountain," which remains the Chinese word for it, and San Francisco was called *Gum San Dai Fow*, "Big City of the Gold Mountain."

People wanted to leave China for many reasons besides the quest for gold. A series of disastrous floods and droughts throughout the nation between 1846 and 1850 resulted in widespread famine. And 1851 marked the beginning of the Taiping Rebellion, a civil war that lasted 13 years and cost the lives of millions. An uprising meant to free the poor from their terrible conditions, the rebellion was finally crushed by the Qing dynasty with the help of Western nations and mercenary soldiers. For most of the nineteenth century, the ordinary people in China suffered greatly from foreign competition and invasions, crime, violence, drug addiction, high taxes, unbearable rents, and unemployment. An estimated 2.5 million people left China over the last half of the 19th century, with about 320,000 coming to North America.

Early settlers came from southern China's Gwangdong Province around the mouth of the Pearl River, an area about the same size as the San Francisco Bay Area. Its provincial capital was Canton (now known as Guangzhou), about a hundred miles northwest of Hong Kong. Because this area is surrounded by high mountains, it is isolated from the rest of China. The Imperial Court in Peking limited early contact with Westerners to this area to prevent the spread of Western influence throughout China. It is estimated that about 80% of the Chinese now living in the United States have roots in Gwangdong Province.

California's Gold Country was a dangerous place during the 1850s. One doctor estimated that one in five miners died within six months after arriving in this state. Easily mined surface deposits were quickly exhausted, and rewards seldom matched the effort and hazard of going underground, digging and dynamiting. There was much greed, violence, and disease due to primitive conditions. The situations and characters were every bit as harsh as those described by the region's most famous miner, Mark Twain.

During the 1850s and 1860s, about four-fifths of the Chinese in California lived in the Gold Country. Even before the Chinese arrived in great numbers, there was much resentment against "foreigners" coming to dig gold. The Chinese quickly learned that it was not a good idea to compete with Caucasians for the most promising sites.

In 1852, the California legislature imposed the first of many discriminatory taxes directed at the Chinese. Many tax collectors were violent and unscrupulous toward them. Between 1852 and 1870, for example, foreign miners' taxes generated over half the state government's revenue. From 1854 to 1872, the testimony of Chinese—along with that of blacks and native Americans—was not admissible in court against whites. (Ironically, the Indians usually thought of the Chinese as another tribe, and left them alone.) The Chinese managed to survive by mining sites that were abandoned by whites or were less promising, persisting long after most whites had given up and abandoned the Gold Country. By 1873, the Chinese had become the largest ethnic group among the miners. Some of their mines continued to operate into the 1880s.

Back from the Gold Country

Because of the extreme labor shortage in San Francisco, conditions were more hospitable there. One of the biggest problems for the early settlers was the small number of women in the young boomtown. In the 1850 census, there were only two women among the 791 Chinese in San Francisco. Women of all races contributed only 8% of the total population of the city, which grew from 6,000 in September 1849 to over 25,000 in just four months. Very few of the would-be millionaires who came here wanted to be bogged down with the everyday chores of cooking and laundry.

There was a Chinese restaurant in San Francisco as early as July 1849. Chinese were much in demand as cooks and domestics in San Francisco, and were often paid more than whites who held the same positions. Caucasians were quick to learn that Chinese food was an excellent value, being both nutritious and flavorful. Chinese restaurants flourished, and to this day are a popular attraction. (We are a grand restaurant town with over 3,200 restaurants. San Franciscans spend more per capita dining out than residents of any other city in America by a wide margin.)

The Chinese fit the restaurant trade well because celebrating and sharing food is very important in Chinese culture. Because famine and overpopulation plagued our history, we have learned to emphasize the joy of good food. Almost any excuse will do for holding a banquet. Another reason for the Chinese involvement with food was that the American diet seemed strange or even somewhat barbaric to many newly arrived Chinese. Vegetables grown here were hardly recognizable to them, and they were shocked at the huge slabs of meat brought to the table uncarved. The Chinese preferred to have food products with which they were familiar shipped from their homeland.

To the Laundry!

Then as now, there was a shortage of fresh water in much of California. Mexican and Indian women provided laundry service at a place called Washer Woman's Lagoon, a body of fresh water at the foot of Russian Hill in what is now the Marina District, west of Chinatown. Considering that it cost $8 to get a dozen shirts done—when an average month's wage was about $12—laundry was a very expensive service for some and a luxury for others.

One way of dealing with this problem was to wear clothes until they wore out or became so offensive that the wearer and his companions could no longer stand it. Legend has it that to cut expenses some men actually put their dirty laundry on clipper ships to Hawaii or Hong Kong. This was a less than ideal solution because it took three to six months to get it back. The Chinese were quick to exploit this market. Many were badly in need of employment, as they had been squeezed out of the Gold Country by the foreign miners' tax, and the laundry provided an income. Requirements were few, investment minimal: a washtub, fresh water, washboard, and soap. Location was not an important factor because the laundry people provided pick-up and delivery service. Often, two laundrymen shared the same premises, one operating in the day and the other at night. By 1852, the price for laundry had dropped considerably, and the tradition of the Chinese laundry was underway. By some estimates, 30% of the Chinese in America were employed in the laundry business by 1920.

Because of the demand for new clothes, an enterprising young man named Levi Strauss used tent material to create durable pants which were the ancestor of blue jeans. The company that bears his name is still based in San Francisco and is now the world's largest garment manufacturer. Indeed, the garment industry is San Francisco's second largest, following tourism. Over 200 garment factories flourish throughout Chinatown and in other locations in the city.

OTHER MEANS OF EMPLOYMENT

In the 1850s and 1860s the Chinese were instrumental in developing the agricultural and fishing industries in Northern California, applying their ancient expertise on land and sea. They added hundreds of millions of dollars to the value of California property by reclaiming land in the Sacramento River Delta area. Many Chinese were employed by the Hungarian Count Harazthy, considered the father of the California wine industry. They worked in all phases of winemaking because of their reliability and willingness to work for less than whites. Using their mining experience, Chinese laborers dug limestone caves for cellaring the wine. This industry was to add far more wealth to the state's economy than gold mining. The supply of Chinese workers in the wine country in the Napa and Sonoma valleys dwindled during the Anti-Chinese hysteria of the 1870s, and especially after the Exclusion Act of 1882, which drastically reduced Chinese immigration. They were replaced by a new wave of immigrants, the Italians, who were familiar with winemaking.

WORKING ON THE RAILROAD

The most notable contribution of Chinese labor to California's economy is in the construction of the Central Pacific railroad, which was being built eastward to meet up with the Union Pacific coming west from the Omaha area. Between 1863 and 1865 the workers made only 50 miles of progress. Only one in ten men lasted more than a week on the job due to the harsh conditions. Management hired Chinese as an experiment and gave them very menial jobs. The efficient Chinese workers numbered 12,000 by the completion of the railroad in 1869. Because of the barrier of the Sierra Nevada Mountains, the anticipated meeting place was to be the California-Nevada border. By mid-1868, the Central Pacific broke through the Sierra barrier. The march across Nevada was much easier. By January 1869, the Central Pacific had broken through to the Great Salt Lake Basin, while the Union Pacific was just emerging from the Rockies. Unlike the white crews, the Chinese had to provide their own food, and they worked from sunrise to sunset, six days a week. The Chinese ate vegetables and rice, a healthier diet than that of their white counterparts, who often developed scurvy because of the lack of fresh vegetables and vitamin C in their diet. The Chinese drank Chinese tea instead of contaminated water, which also contributed to their relatively better health. To this day, many Chinese people prefer to drink boiled water instead of cold water.

Although neither the railroads nor the government kept safety records, other historical evidence indicates that the railroad effort might have cost at least 1,500 Chinese lives. Near the end of construction, the railroad workers were able to complete 10 miles and 56 feet of track in 12 hours, a record that stood until mechanical track layers were invented. The two lines finally met at Promontory Point near Ogden, Utah, on May 10, 1869.

The Chinese were excluded from the closing ceremony at Promontory Point because of the discrimination that existed. E. B. Crocker, brother of railroad baron Charles Crocker, did mention their contribution in one sentence of a speech celebrating the event in Sacramento: "I wish to call your minds to that early completion of this railroad we have built has been in large measure due to that poor, despised class of laborers called Chinese, to the fidelity and industry they have shown."

The Exclusion Act

The great economic boom that many speculators believed would follow the completion of the railroad never did occur. In fact, there were hard times throughout America in the 1870s. The railroad did simplify transportation for unemployed workers from the east, making it easier for them to migrate to California, which increased the competition for jobs.

By 1870 San Francisco had become the fifth leading manufacturing city in America, with about half the jobs in manufacturing held by Chinese. The Chinese differed from other immigrants in that they thought of themselves as visitors rather than settlers, and they maintained close ties to their families and native villages. Most came with the goal of providing for their families in China, and hoped to save enough to return to buy land or set up as merchants in China. They were willing to work long hours at low pay to achieve these goals.

In the 1870s, the Chinese became a convenient scapegoat for demagogues seeking political power who blamed them for taking jobs from non-Chinese workers. Several riots resulted in the burning of Chinese businesses. California cities like Eureka, Truckee, Redlands, and Chico expelled all Chinese. San Francisco's Chinatown and Chinatowns in major cities provided a refuge from violence and racism throughout the United States.

The growing hostility to Chinese throughout the country led to Congress passing the Chinese Exclusion Act of 1882. Under the act, the only Chinese permitted to enter were foreign-born wives and children of American citizens of Chinese ancestry. The Exclusion Act was made even stricter with the Scott Act of 1888, and tightened up even more in following years. The Immigration Act of 1924 finally wiped out all rights of wives and children to enter. The Chinese are the only ethnic group that has ever been specifically barred from entering the United States.

The Chinese did not passively accept the provisions of the exclusion laws. Like other ethnic groups, Chinese civic organizations fought legal battles for decades to achieve equality in the United States. Many have suggested that the Exclusion Act might have been called the "Extermination Act." It served its purpose well: from a peak of a 132,000 population in 1882, the Chinese population in the United States declined to about 62,000 by 1920. No doubt this decline would have been much more precipitous had it not been for the earthquake in San Francisco in 1906.

Portsmouth Square in 1906. The Fairmont Hotel (at top) was under construction.

The firestorm that swept through San Francisco after the quake destroyed all the records of citizenship for the Western United States. This made it very difficult for officials to challenge Chinese claims of citizenship. By some estimates, every Chinese woman would have given birth to an average of eight hundred children for all the claims of citizenship to be legitimate.

Men who returned to China often reported the birth of fictitious sons, creating a market in what became known as "paper sons," which enabled these younger men to come to the United States. They were sons on paper only, and citizenship papers became a negotiable instrument.

In 1910, the U.S. Immigration and Naturalization Service (INS) began using Angel Island, the largest island in the San Francisco Bay, as a quarantine center. For Chinese, the name was a bitter irony. They were detained there routinely for a few days, and in some cases for months or even as long as two or three years. They were confined to their barracks and a small exercise yard. My mother was one of the last of the many thousands who spent varying lengths of time there before the facility closed in 1940 after a fire.

The INS interrogated "paper sons and daughters" for long hours about the details of their adopted families and villages, in an intimidating effort to sift out illegal immigrants. A few wrong or inconsistent answers could lead to immediate deportation. I greatly admire the courage of all the people who endured this to make a better life for themselves. Unfortunately, some people could not handle the stress and committed suicide rather than wait out the chance to land in the city. Many wrote moving poems of anguish and hope on the walls.

My own family story illustrates a typical case of how Chinese could gain entry to the United States. My father and mother both came to America with purchased documents. Inspired by the success of other men in his village who had come to America, my father left China at age 17. His dream was to earn enough money to return to China to open a grocery store. His first destination was the Philippines, where he worked long hours at a variety of jobs, and learned the art of cooking. After six years of work, his dream of returning remained unattainable. For $1,200 he purchased papers declaring him to be Ricardo Torres, a citizen of the Philippines, which were then a U.S. territory. It must have been a bit of a stretch for a Chinese to be known as Ricky Torres, but the name served its purpose and gained him the official right to enter.

上問

你夫婦也若

幾時出世

保大夫傳边廈人氏

你大夫氣時娶妻

在边廈娶

点樣娶

下答

麥世璋平涌係

宣統三年正月廿八日午時出世　全年共廿六歲

保雲海縣子江村雷社人氏

民國九年胃祁一日聖

在花轎為边先娶

術問俗例三叩九禮，吹普閜鼓，花轎迎娶

Larry Mak's father took notes to help his wife answer questions at Angel Island during her detainment. This is a page illustrating typical questions on top, with appropriate answers on the bottom.

He made his way to Oakland, California, in 1927, after contacting relatives from his village in Canton in advance. They helped him to get established by giving him job leads. He worked in Chinese restaurants for several years, starting at the bottom busing tables and working his way up. By 1930, he had opened his own restaurant, New China, on Eighth Street in Oakland. Lunch was 25 cents including salad, bread, coffee, and dessert. Years later, he opened another restaurant, New Eastern Cafe. I remember that as a child I took naps in what was known as the rice room, a closet where 100-pound bags of rice were stored.

My mother was selected as my father's bride by relatives in China, and as a young 18-year-old she journeyed to America in 1940 to begin a new life. Although it was a dream come true for her to come to the United States, she first spent 41 days on Angel Island in a degrading and painful stay. She recalls, "There was a big room with bunk beds. Several tens of women lived in one room." Weeks before her interview with the immigration service officials, Mother spent her time talking with others in the yard surrounding her living quarters. It was a prison to her, and she was frightened by the officers from the INS. These officers interrogated the Chinese men and women at length. She was quizzed for a few hours, all in one day. Husbands and wives who traveled to San Francisco were interrogated separately, and if their answers did not coincide to the satisfaction of the officials, they faced a return trip to China.

During the early 1950s, new laws allowed the Chinese to go to the government, admit that they were paper sons, and become completely legal citizens without penalty. Dad did this so that each of his children could have a Chinese surname. At the last minute, however, he decided to thank the family that helped him to the United States, so he changed his name to Richard Fong-Torres. The Chinese Exclusion Act was not fully repealed until the 1965 Civil Rights Act. Chinese are now on an equal legal footing with other ethnic groups. The current quota for Chinese immigration is 40,600 per year.

Since 1965, there has been a great wave of new immigrants from Hong Kong, Taiwan, and other parts of China and Southeast Asia. Our Chinatown is a bustling place that still gives newcomers a place to start in America, remaining a cultural oasis for thousands of Chinese-Americans, as it has been for over 125 years.

Those interested in learning more about the fascinating history of Chinatown should visit the Chinese Historical Society at 650 Commercial Street. It is a museum containing artifacts of the first Chinese to journey to San Francisco and a wide collection of books on

Ricardo Torres and Joe Tung Low, author's parents on wedding day, 1940.

related subjects. The **Chinese Cultural Center,** located on the third floor of the Holiday Inn in Chinatown, carries books and presents activities related to the Chinese culture, such as art exhibits and demonstrations throughout the year. The **East Wind Bookstore** at **633 Vallejo Street** carries a huge assortment of books on Chinese history, culture, and food, and has an art gallery upstairs. The Chinatown branch of the San Francisco Public Library is located at 1135 Powell Street. These sites are all worth a short detour from the exact route outlined on the map.

CHAPTER 2

*We like to begin our tours by walking up **Washington Street** and into **Portsmouth Square,** the most historical spot in San Francisco. This is where San Francisco began as a city in the 1830s, so it is appropriate to pause here with our tour guests to give a historical narration and reflect on years past. The area east of Portsmouth Square was once prime waterfront property, a shallow cove called Yerba Buena by the Hispanic settlers, extending approximately to where Montgomery Street is today. Yerba Buena Cove was a favorite anchorage for ships that visited the bay because it was protected from the wind by Nob Hill and Telegraph Hill. The cove began disappearing long ago, as it was filled in and buildings were constructed on the fill (over one-third of the entire San Francisco Bay has been filled in since the 1850s).*

PORTSMOUTH SQUARE AREA & COMMERCIAL STREET

The first Anglo-Saxon settler in this city was an Englishman named William Richardson. On June 25, 1835, Richardson, a whaling ship captain, pitched a tent at what is now 827–43 Grant Avenue. A few months later he built a permanent wooden structure at this location, the first house to be built on the site of the future city of San Francisco. Richardson was the port commissioner for Mexico, collecting taxes and tariffs for the Mexican government. A few years later, he received a land grant for what is today's Sausalito, where tax evaders took refuge across the bay to the north.

Portsmouth Square is as old as the city of San Francisco. The town was first surveyed in 1839 by civil engineer Jean J. Vioget. Vioget designed a city plaza facing Yerba Buena Cove where the ships were unloaded, and named the streets after historically prominent men. By 1846 there were approximately two hundred people living in Yerba Buena. The small blocks and narrow streets laid out in the original survey are still a part of today's Chinatown. In fact, Portsmouth Square has always been the same size as it is now, not quite a full block.

On July 9, 1846, Captain John Montgomery and 70 soldiers and marines came ashore from the USS *Portsmouth* and marched to the Mexican Customs House. A lieutenant read a proclamation prepared by Captain Montgomery claiming the territory for the United States. Accompanied by a 21-gun salute from the Portsmouth, the troops took down the Mexican flag and raised the Stars and Stripes, and it has been flying here ever since. Soon after, a street along the embarcadero (Spanish for "wharf") area was named after Montgomery.

By the end of July 1846, Sam Brannan arrived on the USS *Brooklyn*, along with 238 other Mormons. Their arrival practically doubled the population of Yerba Buena. Brannan, 26 years old and a sharp dresser, quickly became one of the most visible local citizens. His purpose in coming here to was escape the religious persecution of the United States, and he was supposed to rendezvous with Mormon leader Brigham Young, who stopped in Salt Lake City instead. After six months at sea, Brannan was not about to set off again, and settled in the village by the bay.

The Mormons were disappointed with their new home because it was cold and foggy. Like many first-time visitors here, they were surprised at the cool, overcast weather in the summertime. At that time much of the city was made up of sand dunes with few trees. Yerba Buena officially became San Francisco on January 30, 1847. Lieutenant Washington A. Bartlett, the appointed *alcalde* (Spanish for "mayor"), wanted it changed from Yerba Buena to San Francisco as an easy identification with the bay of the same name.

Sam Brannan started the city's first newspaper, *California Star,* and on May 12, 1848, announced the discovery of gold by marching down Montgomery Street to Portsmouth Square with vials of gold dust. One of his reporters investigated the rumors that people were paying their bills with gold dust in Sutter's Fort, now the site of Sacramento, the state capital. Legend has it that he opened well-stocked mining supply stores in San Francisco and Sutter's Fort to cash in on the gold rush. Brannan's announcement, along with another newspaper's (the *Californian*'s headline was "GOLD! GOLD! GOLD!" on May 19, 1848) set off the largest peacetime migration in United States history.

From the very beginning, this has been a city that likes to celebrate. It was especially true after the gold rush when there were many bachelors residing here, with few forms of entertainment available. Consequently, in 1851 we had approximately 500 bars in San Francisco for a population of 25,000 people, or one bar for every 50 inhabitants. One of the most popular bars was located on the site of today's Holiday Inn-Chinatown/Financial District on Kearny Street. It was called the Jenny Lind Theatre, named after a well-known Swedish songstress who never actually came to San Francisco. When the city bought the theater's property to build a Hall of Justice, there was a massive demonstration across the street at Portsmouth Square protesting the razing of the Jenny Lind.

TODAY'S PORTSMOUTH SQUARE

Today's Portsmouth Square is indeed a hub of activity. There are few other outdoor places in the United States where you will encounter so many people packed into such a small area. On the upper level, men gather around card tables on the east side of the park to play Chinese chess or

Russian poker. Others soak in the sun as they read or visit with friends. Children play on the lower-level playground. Mothers and grandmothers keep a watchful eye on children playing in the sandbox and on the swing sets. In the early mornings you may observe men and women practicing *tai chi*, a graceful and peaceful form of martial arts exercise with its roots in China's native Taoist philosophy and religion.

BUDDHA'S UNIVERSAL CHURCH

720 Washington Street
Detour for a moment to cross the street from Portsmouth Square near the corner of Washington and Kearny. Here we have the **Buddha's Universal Church**, at **720 Washington Street**, built on the site of a former nightclub. The church's congregation purchased the nightclub in 1951 and incorrectly guessed that a mere $500 remodeling was all that was needed for reopening. After the papers were signed, the city condemned the building because three of its four walls were structurally unsound, and the church had orders to tear it down. This naturally created a huge financial problem for the congregation, and they put their heads together to find a solution. It took over 11 years of hard work by volunteers to rebuild the church, and it became lovingly known as the "Church of a Thousand Hands." Thomas Chinn, in his fascinating history of Chinese-Americans, *Bridging the Pacific*, reports that architect Worley Wong, of the Campbell and Wong architectural firm, had to study Buddhism before he could begin work on the church plans.

Today the church is especially busy around Chinese New Year when a bilingual play is produced and open for several weeks during the new year festivities. Other activities at the church include weddings which can be conducted bilingually.

EMPEROR NORTON—
AND CHANG

On the same side of the street as the Universal Buddhist Church, another drama unfolds. I always look for my Chinese friend, known in the neighborhood simply as Chang. She is a thin, elderly, woman, who dresses in a traditional Chinese jacket and blue pants, and often wears a Chinese straw hat. At first glance, she looks like a frail grandmother. Closer observation will reveal one of the most colorful and energetic characters in Chinatown. For example, her standard greeting to me is: "Shirley! Shirley! Shirley! You're number one."

Almost every morning, Chang can be seen in front of the parking lot that she manages. Parking is a very scarce commodity in Chinatown, and her lot fills up quickly in the mornings. In order to increase the number of available spaces in her lot, Chang monopolizes the street parking. On many occasions, my tour groups and I double up in laughter as we watch her scamper up or down the street with a "No Parking" or "Construction Zone" sign on her small but obviously strong shoulder. She drops these signs down on open spaces in order to hold them for HER customers. Believe me, you won't want to park on Chang's side of the street when she is around. I have seen her chase away many burly truck drivers with her rolled up newspaper and staccato Cantonese. I suspect that the city maximizes its revenue by allowing Chang to operate the way she does. Throughout the day, Chang feeds the parking meters faithfully with her pocketful of coins.

Chang is not as unusual as might seem at first glance. San Francisco has a long history of tolerance for people who march to the beat of a different drummer, whether they're heroes or eccentrics: it's our "Emperor Norton tradition." Joshua Abraham Norton was an Englishman who came to San Francisco in 1849 from South Africa, and by 1853 had amassed about $250,000 as a merchant and speculator in real estate and commodities. He risked this entire fortune by trying to corner the rice market. Norton was still accumulating his hoard when a ship loaded with rice entered the bay. Prices collapsed, and he lost everything. Penniless and with his life in shambles, Norton left town to regroup.

Several months later, he showed up on Montgomery Street in a military uniform with epaulets, a plumed hat, and a cane. He stopped by the office of the *San Francisco Bulletin* and issued a proclamation declaring that henceforth he was to be known as Norton I, Emperor of the United States and Protector of Mexico. The *Bulletin* printed his proclamation, and the city of San Francisco went along with the joke of its "ruler" for more than 25 years.

The Emperor had 50-cent promissory notes printed that were due in 1880. His notes were widely accepted by merchants throughout the city. When his Napoleonic uniform became worn, the city government actually budgeted for purchase of a new outfit for him. Essentially an entertainer, he gave the city a bargain for its money. He conducted himself with the dignity expected of an emperor and rarely overstayed his welcome. Knowing just how far to push his luck and credit, Norton drew the fine line between being an entertaining eccentric and a candidate for lengthy confinement to a mental institution.

Norton had a habit of writing entertaining letters to editors filled with wild notions. Two of his "crackpot" ideas were to build the Golden Gate Bridge from Marin, and the Bay Bridge from Oakland to the city where he reigned. He was so obsessed with building the Bay Bridge that at one point he presented a worthless check in the amount of $3.5 million to the city to finance construction of the bridge. (It cost over 10 times that amount to complete these projects in the 1930s.) There was an irresistible humanitarianism in his madness, too. One of his proclamations called for placing a Christmas tree for children at Union Square, a practice that continues to this day, and he attended both Christian and Jewish services to promote religious harmony. Norton lived near Chinatown, and he once defused an anti-Chinese mob by standing in front of them reciting the Lord's Prayer. When Norton died suddenly in 1879, he was waving to tourists on a cable car on California Street.

He had become such a popular figure that more than 10,000 admirers attended his funeral. San Francisco still has Emperor Norton festivals and even has an Emperor Norton Hotel on Post Street. If Emperor Norton was still alive, he might well be working alongside Chang.

Take a few steps back up into Portsmouth Square, to the northwest corner. Reflect in front of the **Robert Louis Stevenson** monument. Stevenson, the novelist and poet, lived with his wife nearby on Bush Street between 1879 and 1880. He loved to sit and watch the ships out on the bay, and became a great friend of the Chinese people at a time when it was unusual for a Caucasian to befriend a Chinese person. No doubt he was rewarded by sharing some fine Chinese meals with his friends. The ship that is on top of the monument is a replica of the *Hispaniola,* from his

Men relaxing on benches in front of pagoda-style building at Portsmouth Square.

famous pirate saga *Treasure Island,* and the inscription is from his "A Christmas Sermon."

If you stood here in 1907 or 1908 and looked around, the scenery would have been very similar to what you see today with a few exceptions of high-rise buildings.

When my mother arrived in San Francisco from China in 1940, Portsmouth Square was quite a different scene:

dirty and dilapidated, looking quite a bit like a vacant lot with very few trees. It was not landscaped as it is today, and the card tables were not in place until the 1970s, when the city improved the landscaping and the facilities. One of my staff tour guides, Dorothy Quock, remembers: "When I was about six years old, I tagged along with my brothers to shine shoes, charging five cents. Sometimes the Caucasian customers paid my brothers and gave a few cents tip to me as well!"

But Portsmouth Square is especially beautiful today, thanks to a recent sprucing up of the area. There is an inviting rest area next to a modern elevator, complete with a Chinese-style pagoda roof with turned-up eaves. (The four-level parking garage directly beneath is still one of the best places to park in Chinatown; the entrance to the garage is on the street level of Kearny Street.)

For a quick review of the history of the immediate area, pause in front of the **plaque** located between the upper and lower levels of the park, by the stairs. Read about the contributions of William Richardson and Sam Brannan, and the demonstration protesting the destruction of the Jenny Lind Theatre across the street from Portsmouth Square.

On the Clay Street side of the lower level of this park, there is a bronze **plaque** commemorating Andrew Halladie, inventor of the famed cable cars. Halladie had a wire rope manufacturing business on Powell Street, and his product was used with mining equipment for pulling carts up out of mines and other operations. One rainy day in the winter of 1869, Halladie witnessed a horse-drawn cart accident and determined that there had to be a better way to get up and down our steep streets and hills. The answer came in August 1873, when the first cable car line ran from the Clay Street side of Portsmouth Square up to Jones Street.

Halladie's invention also contributed to the development of Chinatown. Although many Chinese lived in the Chinatown area from the earliest days of the city, they were also dispersed throughout San Francisco. After the cable cars came into service, many non-Chinese residents moved out of what had been the core of the city to live on the newly accessible hills, using the cars to commute back and forth from the central area. This migration roughly coincided with the growing resentment and violence toward the Chinese that arose during the 1870s. As Caucasians moved out, the Chinese moved in to be closer to their own people for security and protection. What was once the heart of the city became Chinatown. To learn more about the cable cars, you could take a small detour from our route and visit the free Cable Car Museum, just four blocks uphill from Portsmouth Square, at the corner of Washington and Mason Streets.

The Clay Street cable car line was the first in the city. Cable cars contributed to the development of Chinatown.

On the west side of the park, Walter U. Lum Place is a narrow street named after the first president of the Chinese-American Citizens Alliance. Lum was a civil rights leader, and it is believed that this is the *first* street in America named after a Chinese person. Another Asian-American civil rights organization, **Chinese for Affirmative Action** (CAA) at **7 Walter U. Lum Place,** was organized in 1969. Its purpose is to promote equal opportunity in employment and education for the community, and it keeps a close eye on legislation relating to the civil rights of the Chinese. The building that houses CAA was a communications center for Chinese revolutionaries in 1910. A young school girl brought messages to the revolutionary leader Sun Yat-sen and his cohorts there, sometimes making several trips a day.

When you are finished looking around Portsmouth Square, walk back to **Washington Street** and turn left. This area was the food district before the earthquake in 1906. **Wentworth Alley** across the street was called "Salt Fish Alley" and my tour leader George Mew's father operated a salted-fish store there. I like to stop at **Mow Fung Wholesale Produce Market** at **733 Washington,** which has been a family business since 1912. This market carries the freshest Chinese vegetables, from baby bok choy, Chinese long beans, and watercress, to gigantic wintermelons. Mow Fung distributes to many Chinese restaurants in the community, and their produce comes from as near as the San Francisco peninsula and as far as South America. Oftentimes when wintermelon and bittermelon are not available elsewhere, you can find it at Mow Fung. For something special to take home, I recommend picking up some fresh water chestnuts or lemon grass, which do not require immediate refrigeration. Mow Fung carries excellent fresh fruit as well. We will cover Chinese produce in Chapter 12.

Right next to the Mow Fung produce market is the **Silver Restaurant,** at **737 Washington,** where we are captivated by the display of hanging roast ducks and chickens, the trays of marinated duck feet, rolls of stark white rice noodles sprinkled with dried shrimp, and long deep-fried Chinese bread. It is a sight to watch a skilled worker chop up a duck with his sharp cleaver in a matter of minutes.

Bank of Canton, former Chinese Telephone Exchange.

Early in my tour career, I called the health department to question its standards for Chinatown's hanging ducks and chickens, as I wanted to make sure this was a safe way to treat food. I was told to "leave the Chinese people alone. If you don't like 'em, don't buy 'em. They have been doing this for years, not only in San Francisco but in the Orient. It's traditional and the Chinese have never complained about getting sick from it."

The Silver restaurant is a great place to stop in for a hot bowl of *jook*, Chinese rice gruel, also known as *congee.* The chef scoops an order of jook from a large vat, heats it up in a smaller pot, and tops the bowl with your choice of meat or poultry, and a bit of green onion and soy sauce. Jook is considered Chinese comfort food.

It's fun to sit by the open kitchen to watch the chefs cook up your order of jook, noodles, or dumplings. Ducks and chickens are roasted in the kitchen downstairs, and one can hear woks sizzling up stir-fried noodles and other delicious entrees. The Silver Restaurant is open 24 hours a day, for a soothing meal at any time.

Commercial Street is one of the last brick-paved streets in San Francisco.

While you are still on Grant and Washington, detour across the street for another photo opportunity: the **Bank of Canton** at **743 Washington Street,** known foremost as the former Chinese Telephone Exchange. This was probably the only foreign language telephone exchange in the United States. Operators had to speak five dialects of Chinese as well as English. They also had to remember the phone numbers of the clients, because most of the customers asked for people by name since they felt it was rude to refer to people as numbers. The Telephone Exchange closed in 1949 when it was replaced by rotary dialing. This site was also the location of Sam Brannan's *California Star* newspaper. The Bank of Canton purchased and restored the building in 1960.

Return to **Grant Avenue** and make a left turn on Grant, and walk south toward **Clay Street.** Serious cooks will want to stop in at **The Wok Shop** at **804 Grant.** They

Yerba Buena Cove in 1852.

have a complete selection of cooking utensils, cookbooks, and even packaged Chinese-vegetable seeds for those who'd like to try growing their own. (For more about cooking utensils, see the cooking section in this book.) When you reach Clay Street, cross and continue about a half block to our next stop at **the corner of Commercial and Grant.**

Grant Avenue is the oldest street in our city. The Hispanic settlers called it *Calle de la Fundación* or Foundation Street. When the Americans took over, the name was changed to Dupont Street in honor of one of the officers on the USS *Portsmouth*. After the 1906 earthquake, the name of the street was again changed—to Grant Avenue—in honor of President Ulysses Grant. For most of its history, Grant Avenue was a two-way street, and there were many accidents because of its narrowness. Some older Chinese in the community still prefer to call it "Dupont Gai" (*gai* means "street" in Chinese) because there is no equivalent sound to "r" in the Cantonese language.

When we get to the corner of **Grant and Commercial Streets,** we step just around the corner to escape the busy foot traffic on Grant Avenue. Other than on Market Street, this is the only spot in the city where you can get a clear

These pictures are two halves of a view from Clay Street.

view of the Ferry Building. Commercial Street was not part of the original survey of the town. Early settlers created Commercial Street so that cargo could be hauled up from Yerba Buena Cove to Grant Avenue. On the corner two blocks down the hill on the right side of the street, the British Hudson Bay Company established an office in 1841. From this point, Long Wharf once extended two thousand feet out into the bay to provide room for all the ships to anchor and unload.

After the Gold Rush, Yerba Buena Cove quickly became filled with abandoned ships. Many of the ships were derelict vessels that had barely made the trip, and often their crews and captains simply abandoned them to seek fortune in the Gold Country. Many of the ships that did leave dumped unwanted cargo into the bay before setting sail. Standing at this spot gives you a good idea of how much of San Francisco's financial district is on bay fill. One of the many contributions of Chinese laborers was to round off some of the steeper hills in the city, digging away soil and rock used to fill in Yerba Buena Cove.

Commercial Street, one of the last brick-paved streets in San Francisco, is now lined with wholesale businesses, mostly garment shops. Pasta lovers may want to stop at the

National Noodle Company at **739–41 Commercial** for some excellent dry wide noodles. Although this is a Chinese-operated business, most of its clients are actually Japanese restaurateurs who order *soba,* the thin noodles made from buckwheat and used primarily in Japanese cuisine. National Noodle Company also specializes in the rounded, thicker noodles called *udon.*

Commercial Street is an exciting street for history buffs. Stroll down to the **Chinese Historical Society Museum** at **650 Commercial Street.** The museum is open from noon to 4 p.m., Tuesday through Saturday. They have a great selection of books and some reasonably priced gifts. The museum is free, although donations are appreciated. Next door is the **Pacific Heritage Museum** at **608 Commercial Street,** located on the site of the original San Francisco Mint built in 1854. You can look at the vaults and a historical display of the building. The museum features changing exhibitions on economic and cultural exchanges across the Pacific. It is open Monday through Friday from 10 a.m. to 4 p.m., and admission is free. Around the corner at **420 Montgomery Street** is the **Wells Fargo History Room.** The display cases here tell the story of Wells Fargo's contribution to the Gold Rush. This museum is open from 9 a.m. to 5 p.m., Monday through Friday.

In the next chapter we will explore another important area that helped to shape Chinatown in its early days. From **Commercial Street,** walk uphill to **Grant Avenue.** Make a left turn and continue a half block to **Sacramento Street.**

CHAPTER 3

Sacramento Street is best known as Tong Yun Gai, which means "Chinese Street." Dating back to the earliest days of the gold rush era, this was the first street where Chinese were allowed to rent rooms. Unlike many other ethnic neighborhoods in this and other cities, where many members of the original groups eventually moved away, Chinatown has remained Chinese, expanding from its original base.

SACRAMENTO STREET: EDUCATION, TRADITIONS, FESTIVALS

Both my uncle by marriage, Henry Chew, and one of our tour leaders, George Mew, were born and raised in the same building at 725 Sacramento Street. George came from a large family, and in those days (1920s) living conditions were very cramped. When a family moved out of a unit, relatives would move in. Eventually, the Mew family took over the entire building.

It was not uncommon for children to go to American school in the morning followed by Chinese school in the evening. For example, George went to St. Mary's school on Clay and Stockton and then to a Chinese-language school. operated by a district association, every night from five to eight o'clock. My sister, brothers, and I attended Chinese school throughout our youth, across the bay in Oakland's Chinatown. After school, I helped out at our family restaurant. Many people have asked if it wasn't too stressful for kids to go to two schools in one day and work in the family business. I did not know otherwise and never complained publicly. From high school, we were expected to continue our education in college, no questions asked.

The **Nam Kue Chinese School,** located at **755 Sacramento Street,** was established in 1925. It was created and operated by the Fook Yum Tong district association. After the 1906 earthquake, Chinatown ceased to be a bachelor society and for the first time there were many children in Chinatown. Chinese schools were developed to give the children a uniquely Chinese education so that they could return to China with a knowledge of their culture. In fact, many children did return to China and contributed greatly to the country's development as bilingual business and professional people.

The **Chinese Chamber of Commerce** at **728–30 Sacramento Street** was established in 1908 as a compromise to settle a bitter economic feud between the Sam Yup and Say Yup district associations. As a result of this feud, many Chinese businesses went bankrupt due to boycotts and other disruptions. The Sam Yups were merchants from the areas closest to Canton, while Say Yup people were laborers and restaurant employees from the southern area of the Pearl River Delta. The purpose of the Chinese Chamber of Commerce was to promote the economic interests of Chinatown. Today it is considered the most powerful political arm of the Chinese community and continues to be very active in our cultural and economic life.

Each year the Chinese Chamber of Commerce co-sponsors the Miss Chinatown U.S.A. Pageant and the Chinese New Year parade.

FONDEST
FESTIVAL MEMORIES

While the Miss Chinatown Pageant is a modern local innovation, the Chinese New Year festival has ancient roots. Festivals are a very special part of Chinese culture. As a child, I sensed a special day was around the corner whenever Mom busied herself at the sewing machine to make a new dress for me, and when our home kitchen filled with sensational aromas of stir-fried dried shrimp, green onion, minced prawns, fresh water chestnuts, and mushrooms. Mom prepared fillings for one or more varieties of steamed or fried dumplings and pastries. After setting the filling aside, she measured out wheat starch into a large green mixing bowl to which she added boiling water, a little at a time. She pounded down on the bowl of flour and water with her hands to make a dough. It amazed me that she didn't burn herself. Next, she rolled the dough into long thin cylinders, cut them into even-sized pieces, and pressed them into little balls in the palms of her hands. Patiently, she scooped a tablespoon of filling into the center of each wrapper, and deftly wrapped them into pretty little dumplings. Then they were lined in rows on a flour-dusted cookie sheet. After they were cooked, we ate a few, and she had some on hand for visitors or to take to our friends' homes. I imagined back then that all mothers must have spent hours making these wondrous little morsels. I didn't understand why my Caucasian friends' mothers baked cookies!

It seems as though we are always celebrating something. In addition to the American celebrations of birthdays, anniversaries, and national holidays, there is a stream of Chinese festivals. We have many customs and plays on words of tradition and food, so that food is central to our get-togethers. Here are some of the most familiar Chinese celebrations.

CHINESE
NEW YEAR

Chinese New Year usually takes place in late January or early February, depending on the lunar calendar. We celebrate for two full weeks. Probably more food is consumed during the period of celebrating the New Year than any other time in the year. In addition to preparing vast amounts of traditional food for family and friends, food is also cooked for those close to us who have died. The house is cleaned thoroughly and bills are always paid up— modern America must love such Chinese customs.

On New Year's Day itself, we are not supposed to wash our hair lest we wash away good luck for the new year. Red clothing is conspicuous during this festive occasion. Red is considered a bright, happy color, sure to bring the wearer a sunny and bright future. Children and unmarried friends, as well as close relatives, are given *lai see*, little red envelopes with crisp one-dollar bills inserted, for good fortune. Although Larry Mak, a Wok Wiz tour leader, is older than me, I give him lai see year after year. As long as he is unmarried, he is considered a child.

Prior to Chinese New Year's Day, we decorate our living rooms with vases of pretty blossoms, platters of oranges and tangerines, and a plate with eight varieties of dried sweet fruit. On walls and doors are poetic couplets, happy wishes written on red paper. These wishes sound better than the typical fortune-cookie messages. For instance, "May you enjoy continuous good health," and "May the Star of Happiness, the Star of Wealth, and the Star of Longevity shine on you" are especially positive couplets.

This holiday is shared by millions of people with much zest in Chinatowns throughout the world. The atmosphere in our local Chinatown is colorful and carnival-like. In fact, a carnival does take place right at Portsmouth Square. Street vendors bring out to the sidewalk products associated with the occasion: festive dried goods and candy, flowers and plants, and packets of red envelopes in all sizes and always decorated with calligraphy or characters in gold. The already crowded streets along Stockton and Grant, and perpendicular side streets are packed as competing vendors in nursery trucks park and sell, on the spot, flowering plants and colorful blossoms of quince and other flowers. I enjoy stepping back to soak in the energy of the day.

The Harry Lee family sits down to share a traditional Chinese New Year's dinner.

There are many rituals in the traditional family. I was born in America, but I know my roots and understand how I am expected to behave. When visiting my parents during New Year's, I dress in a bright, happy outfit, and utter not a single negative word. It is believed that appearance and attitude during New Year's sets the tone for the year to come. I bring a bag of the brightest oranges and tangerines available, and the tangerines must have leaves intact. A red envelope with lucky money is placed in the bag. Mom and Dad will give back half the fruits to me, and tuck in one of their own lucky money envelopes. *Note:* etiquette dictates that you must bring a bag of oranges and tangerines and enclose a lai see when visiting family or friends any time during the two-week-long Chinese New Year celebration. Tangerines with leaves intact assure that one's relationship with the other remains secure. For newlyweds, this represents the branching of the couple into a family with many children. You can choose the interpretation that best suits your hopes and dreams.

Our parents, siblings, in-laws, and children gather for the opening of the New Year. We share a dinner with the traditional foods, especially a vegetarian stew called *lo han*

Grandma Lee prepares to pray to the kitchen god.

jai, a whole fish to represent togetherness and abundance, and a chicken for prosperity. There is too much food, but we know better than to complain. Such abundance means that our rice bowls will remain full throughout the year. The majority of the food is prepared the night before so that on New Year's Day nothing is cut up for fear that one might "cut the luck of the New Year." As if it were only yesterday, Mom sets out a platter of homemade Chinese New Year dumplings.

The culmination of our two-week festivities is the spectacular Chinese New Year parade, presented annually by the San Francisco Chinese Chamber of Commerce and corporate sponsors. A magical, crowd pleasing, and color-ful 60-foot dragon, operated by more than 50 dancers, weaves its way from the start of the parade, usually on Market and Second Streets, all the way through the main streets of Chinatown, along Stockton Street, and finally to an ear-popping firecracker-dodging climax at the review-ing-stand area on Kearny and Columbus Avenue. This parade is one of San Francisco's largest celebrations, and over 500,000 people attend, rain or shine. The Chinese New Year must have ear-piercing firecrackers and drum-mers, since they combine to add to the revelry and scare away the evil spirits.

■ MID-AUTUMN, OR MOON FESTIVAL

Wall to wall colorful red-and -gold boxes of moon cakes are on sale in August of each year in Chinatowns all over the world. This is when the Chinese community celebrates the 15th day of the eighth month, the second most important annual Chinese festival in the lunar calendar. Legend has it that on this particular night there is always a full moon. When you look at the moon closely, you may see a three-legged toad that was formerly a beautiful woman, or the impression may be of a rabbit sitting under a tree. Many modern-day Chinese could care less about the origin of this festival—they look forward to the treat of the moon cakes, usually filled with black bean, yellow bean, lotus bean paste, and my least favorite, mixed nuts and fruits. Most of the moon cakes contain a salted duck-egg yolk in the center. The most symbolic moon cakes are those which contain double yolks for double happiness.

The students of Yau Kung Moon kung fu studio wait their turn to perform a lion dance in a Chinatown restaurant.

The San Francisco Police Department lion dancers ward away evil spirits at Chinatown businesses.

The San Francisco Police Department Lion Dance Team performing in front of Tommy Toy's restaurant.

WEDDINGS

If a younger sister marries before her older brothers, she is obliged to buy them pants, a pair of shoes, and socks. I had to go out and buy slacks for my two older brothers and never understood why—I asked one of my cousins recently, and he said it was simply an old Chinese tradition, not to be questioned. He added that the bride is also supposed to give her groom a belt. A Chinese tea ceremony may take place after the church ceremony, at which time the bride is received into her husband's family and showered with gifts of jade, pearls, and gold. She changes into a traditional Chinese dress, and wears all the pieces of jewelry received at the tea ceremony. Manners dictate that the bride wear every piece of jade, pearl, and gold presented to her to the evening's dinner celebration. I think young brides nowadays should have body guards to accompany them to the formal banquet.

At the banquet, the bride, groom, and respective families sit at tables on a raised platform to signify that they are the honored guests. On the wall is the character for double happiness emblazoned in gold. The sumptuous dinner usually includes shark's fin soup, an expensive delicacy that represents prosperity and power. The golden color of the soup represents gold, and long life—may the diners have the power and speed of a shark.

RED EGG
AND GINGER

A Chinese baby's one-month birthday celebration is usually in the form of an afternoon multi-course luncheon. The baby is dressed up, possibly with gifts of jade, gold bracelets, and necklaces. The baby usually sleeps through this party so it is really a celebration for family and friends. In addition to the good food, it gives everyone a chance to look at the newborn child. Hard-boiled eggs, tinted in lucky color red, and golden-colored sliced pickled ginger are always served to guests toward the end of the meal for happiness and prosperity.

DOUBLE-NINE FESTIVAL

On the ninth day of the ninth moon, celebrants of this festival go to hilltops to fly kites and drink chrysanthemum wine. This festival originated during the Han Dynasty, 206 B.C.–A.D. 220, at the height of ancient Chinese civilization. Sentries were sent to the tops of hills to prevent thieves from robbing the graineries filled with the fall harvest. Legend has it that a scholar named Huan Ching was told by a fortune teller to take his family to the top of the hill and drink chrysanthemum wine. For some mysterious reason, when he returned home, all of his cattle and chickens were dead. If Ching had not heeded this warning, he and his family may also have died.

The Double-Nine Festival is now celebrated by flying kites, which were invented in China at least 2,500 years ago, according to records from the Spring and Autumn Period of 722–481 B.C. They were not graceful hobbies or toys then, but were used in war for signaling and communications. One legend even claims that in the Han dynasty a famous warrior flew above the enemy troops in a colossal kite, singing their native folk songs. The troops became so homesick on hearing the songs from the sky that they left the battlefield and abandoned the territory to return home. Today kites come in various sizes and shapes, and are made of nylon, cotton, paper, and wood. Traditional Chinese kites are flying works of art with paintings of legendary heroes and heroines, animals, mythical creatures, bold colors, and intricate designs. If you are interested in Chinese kites, visit **The Chinatown Kite Shop** at **717 Grant Avenue,** with a branch store in the Cannery. To complete this Double-Nine Festival, share some chrysanthemum wine and a banquet.

■ CHINESE FUNERALS IN CHINATOWN

The blaring of a street band or whistling police officers signify that a funeral procession is coming through. The procession begins with a white convertible carrying a portrait of the deceased, followed by the marching band. Sometimes the family members and close friends walk alongside the slow-moving hearse. If the deceased was a well-known member of the Chinese community, the hearse drives by his or her favorite places, for a last visit to Chinatown. Counterfeit money is thrown on the street by the mourners to provide for ancestors and to placate evil spirits that might bother the deceased in the afterlife. It is a ritual for the surviving family members to host a luncheon or dinner, and later distribute money, usually a dollar or less, in a small red envelope so family and friends can buy something sweet to eat, to ameliorate sad feelings.

Tied in with folklore and festivals is the Chinese Horoscope. You can find many books and posters in Chinatown that have some connection to astrology, Chinese style. We ask those who are interested in the horoscope to tell the month and year of their birth, and look up what animal they are according to the Chinese calendar. There are twelve animals in the Chinese lunar calendar, each having associated characteristics. Whether or not one believes in astrology or zodiac signs, it is always fun to learn what animal your birthdate represents.

The Asian legend of astrological signs tells that almost 5,000 years ago Buddha called together all the animals in creation for a meeting but only 12 animals attended. The first to arrive was the rat, followed by the ox, tiger, rabbit, dragon, snake, horse, sheep, monkey, rooster, dog, and boar. In return for their loyalty, Buddha named a year after each one of these animals, in the order that they arrived.

Today it is believed by many Chinese that one's personality and destiny are shaped according to which animal sign one is born under. A person born in the Year of the Snake, for instance, is supposed to possess great wisdom and beauty and is reflective, organized, and alert. People are born in 12 year cycles. Snake people, for instance, were born in 1929, 1941, 1953, 1965, 1977, 1989.

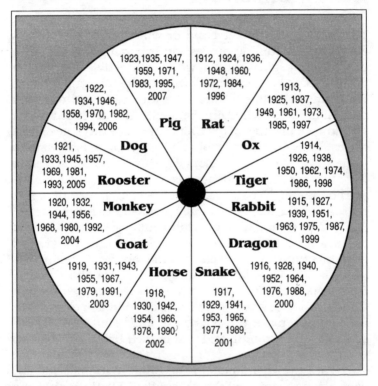

The Chinese, however, take Chinese astrology to heart. It is their belief that a baby's destiny is shaped according to the hour, day, month, and year of its birth.

The chart above indicates animals and characteristics that may be a part of one's personality. Please note that this is for enjoyment, and only an introduction to the field. Serious followers of Chinese astrology, like their Western counterparts, study this subject with great intensity.

YEARS

RAT, MOUSE—

Survivors and quick to adapt to situations and environment. Symbols of wealth because rats are always able to find food, considered a basic form of wealth.

OX, BUFFALO, BULL—

Powerful, stubborn, sensible. Strong and not willing to make too many changes—down to earth and practical.

TIGER—

A charmer and fighter, powerful, protective, and aggressive. A beautiful animal that will attack if his territory is invaded.

RABBIT, HARE—

Quiet and reserved, humble, shy, and withdrawn. An excellent judge of character, can detect sincerity or trouble. Kindhearted and lovable.

DRAGON—

An imaginary animal, the dragon is considered the flashiest and boldest member of the Chinese astrological family. Dragon people are extroverted, generous at heart, determined, and decisive.

SNAKE, SERPENT—

Symbol of medicine and healing, the snake is harmless and peaceful, admired for its beauty. Beautiful and senuous like a snake, intuitive, and intelligent.

Horse—

The saying goes, "healthy as a horse." Strong, speedy; people born in the horse year are tough and hard workers, good talkers, and competitive by nature.

Ram, sheep, goat—

Gentle and wise, the ram is compassionate and not a fighter. A follower rather than a leader, happiest in a crowd, and is best not placed in a position to make decisions.

Monkey—

Intelligent and quick-witted, monkeys are playful and popular, though schemers. They are energetic and develop personal loyalties.

Rooster, hen—

Proud, confident, and bossy, roosters make great managers and leaders. They are assertive, independent, and aggressive, definitely not followers.

Dog—

Loyalty and fidelity are traits of dogs. They are loyal guardians, alert, and intelligent. Active and sociable, ready to mix at get-togethers, and good listeners.

Pig, boar—

Peaceful and ready to retire, the pig is caring and natural, not lazy, but quiet.

After you've looked around, go from the **700 block of Sacramento Street,** return uphill to Grant Avenue, and make a left turn onto **California Street** for the next stretch of the tour.

CHAPTER 4

金
山

*The corner of **Grant and California** combines many of the elements of San Francisco in one spot. Where else can you find cable cars, a cathedral, Chinatown and its pagoda-style buildings, and a view of Nob Hill and the Bay Bridge? This is one of the most photographed areas in the city, although difficult to capture on camera from up close. Two impressive structures here are the pagoda-style buildings on the northwest and southwest corners of the intersection. An interesting story lies behind their existence. We will pause here to discuss the architectural history of Chinatown.*

St. Mary's Square & Grant Avenue / Gateway to Chinatown

Prior to the earthquake in 1906, the Chinese had a negligible impact on the architecture of the city. By one account, at least 75 prefabricated homes here in 1849 were imported from Canton, China. Unfortunately, none of these early homes or pictorial evidence of them survived the many fires that devoured the city between 1849 and 1851.

Chinese laborers and construction workers built **St. Mary's Church** on the **northeast corner of the intersection of Grant and California.** Construction began in 1852 and was completed in 1854. The granite foundation and trim of the church was imported from China.

It was difficult for the Chinese to buy property here. San Francisco permitted racially restrictive real estate covenants until 1947. Those who were able to buy were forced to pay very high prices. By the 1906 earthquake, only about 30 of the 360 parcels of land in Chinatown were owned by Chinese.

Chinatown's very existence was precarious. The second state constitution, adopted in 1879, gave incorporated towns the right to remove Chinese from their boundaries. In 1885 an extensive report submitted to the board of supervisors justified the removal of Chinatown for a long list of economic, moral, and public-health reasons. In 1900 the Board of Health announced an outbreak of bubonic plague in Chinatown. They sent 159 policemen to rope off Chinatown, and prevented any Chinese from leaving. When the Chinese challenged the quarantine in court, it was ruled illegal because the city could produce no evidence of plague in Chinatown.

A private corporation was formed for the purpose of removing the Chinese and Chinatown in 1905. It was called the "United States Improvement and Investment Company." Company spokesman John Partridge proposed to buy Chinatown and relocate the Chinese in a kind of theme park just outside the southern boundary of the city. The new city on the bay was to have all its own facilities and be accessible to tourists. Investors in the company expected to quadruple the value of the land in Chinatown once the Chinese were moved out, because of the rapid growth of the financial district.

Sing Fat Building on the corner of Grant Avenue and California Street typifies San Francisco–style Chinese architecture. Notice the Chinese street lamp.

During the 1906 earthquake and fire storm, much of Chinatown and the rest of the city was nearly leveled. Most of the residents of Chinatown were evacuated to the Presidio, and there was much speculation that the new Chinatown would be in that area. Shortly after the earthquake, the Board of Supervisors appointed a committee to study the relocation of Chinatown. On April 23, 1906, the committee announced that the new Chinatown would be located at Hunter's Point in the southern part of the city.

Needless to say, the Chinese didn't think much of the city's plan. A few of the Chinese merchants who owned property had the foresight to rebuild quickly an area that would be attractive to tourists. Their idea caught on, and was endorsed by the San Francisco Real Estate Board which recommended that Caucasian property owners rebuild their buildings with Oriental and artistic storefronts.

Two Chinese merchants were behind this idea—Tong Bong and Look Tin Eli. Tong Bong owned the building on the northwest corner of Grant and California, and was one of the first antique and art dealers in Chinatown. The building on the southeast corner was a meat market and geneal store owned by Look Tin Eli. Because there were no Chinese architects in San Francisco, both men chose the team of architect T. Paterson Ross and engineer A.W. Burgren to design their buildings. The architects' most important idea was to interpret Chinese architecture while adhering to U.S. building codes and using American-made materials. In doing so, they created a style of architecture unique to San Francisco. Ross and Burgren successfully introduced stylized pagodas and other Chinese motifs as dramatic decorations to the buildings. Although pagodas originated in India, where they were used to house Buddhist shrines, their religious significance was lost in China. Chinese pagodas have captured the imagination of visitors for centuries.

The reconstruction of Chinatown was completed over the next decade and, for the most part, critics were pleased. No one has seriously suggested that Chinatown be moved since its reconstruction, and journalists have been describing it ever since as one of the most fascinating places in North America.

Cross California Street and walk downhill to the steps leading up into **St. Mary's Square.** Walk up into the park. This is one of the few quiet spots in Chinatown. Unlike Portsmouth Square, there are no gaming tables here, and the park is shaded most of the day by the high-rise buildings around it. The park is dominated by the stainless-steel and granite statue of **Dr. Sun Yat-sen,** a man who is considered by many Chinese to be the George Washington of China. Born to a tenant farmer's family near Canton, China, in 1866, as a youth he moved to Hawaii where he was educated and exposed to Western culture. While still a young adult he returned to China to become the first graduate of the British Medical College there.

A statue of Dr. Sun Yat-sen watches over St. Mary's Square.

Dr. Sun was simultaneously appalled by the weakness and ineptness of the Qing dynasty government in China and intrigued by the ideas about government that he had learned in the West. He traveled 1,600 miles from Canton to Beijing to present his ideas for reform to the Imperial Court. After being denied an audience, he dedicated his life to instituting a republican form of government in China. For fifteen years he traveled throughout Europe and North America raising money and support for his cause. Dr. Sun's life was in constant danger. At one point he was captured by Chinese diplomats in Britain and nearly deported in chains. A former teacher persuaded the British government to intervene at the last minute to free him.

Dr. Sun lived secretly in Chinatown during 1910, formed a political party, and started a newspaper that promoted his revolutionary ideas. As noted at Portsmouth Square, the mortuary there served as a communication center for his revolutionary intrigue. When Dr. Sun's revolution succeeded on November 5, 1911, there was a great celebration in Chinatown. He was selected as the first president of the Republic of China, a position that he held for two years. Unfortunately, Dr. Sun was a better orator and fund-raiser than political strategist. His dream of developing a representative democracy was never realized because of the internal strife in China. He died in China in 1925.

Dr. Sun's statue was commissioned by the Works Progress Administration in 1938, and was sculpted by Beniamino Bufano. Many critics consider it one of Bufano's finest works.

The plaque on the opposite side of the park honors Americans of Chinese descent who gave their lives for the U.S. during World Wars I and II. The park provides probably the best view of what is functionally San Francisco's tallest building, the 52 stories of Bank of America.

Continue walking through the park over to Pine Street, turn right and walk back over to Grant Avenue. When you get to the corner, cross Pine. Walk downhill to Bush Street and the **Chinatown Gate** for another dramatic view and photo opportunity. (If you have trouble walking on hills, you may wish to skip this section of our tour.)

The Chinatown Gate was completed in 1970, and was designed by Clayton Lee as part of a design competition. Its inscription "All under heaven is for the good of the people" is from Dr. Sun Yat-sen. The foo dogs that guard the gate are mythical creatures that ward off evil spirits. The fish are a symbol of prosperity and abundance. The dragons at the top are benevolent symbols representing power and fertility. The ball between the dragons represents the earth and ultimate truth.

The gate to Chinatown is aligned with the south, which is considered the most favorable entrance to a city or a building according to the principles of *Feng Shui*. In Cantonese it is pronounced "foong" and "suey." Translated literally the word *feng* means "wind" and *shui* means "water." It reflects ancient traditions that were first codified in the ninth century A.D. by a scholar named Yang Yunsung.

Essentially, Feng Shui has to do with the energy and feel of a place. In a sense it is the earthly counterpart of astrology. Some Chinese believe that the earth's influences explain why two people who may have been born at the exact same moment will have different fates in life. Unlike the heavens, which were beyond the control of man, the forces and influences of the earth could be shaped and influenced by man to control the future.

Practitioners of Feng Shui are called geomancers. The basic tool of the trade is called a Lo P'an, which is a predecessor of the compass. Long before the earth's magnetism was understood, geomancers felt two kinds of

Gateway to Chinatown on Grant Avenue and Bush Street.

energy in the world: *chi,* a beneficial form of energy that meandered gently along irregular paths; and *sha,* an ill-starred form of energy that traveled in straight lines, also recognized as secret arrows with evil impact. The geomancer's job is to maximize the chi and minimize the sha of a given site. One manifestation of this in Chinatown is the turned-up eaves on the buildings throughout the district: their purpose is to ward off sha. The concepts of chi and sha are also used in martial arts and Chinese medicine.

Before dismissing all this as hopeless superstition, please read on for an appreciation of the practical advantages of this ancient body of knowledge. Some of the most successful businesses in San Francisco, such as Tommy Toy's restaurants on Montgomery Street, have been designed by Feng Shui practitioners to give the proprietors a sense of peace and impending prosperity. At the very least, Feng Shui has great influence on real-estate transactions in Asian communities throughout much of the world.

Feng Shui was originally practiced as part of the Taoist religion, although it is now used by Buddhist, Muslim, and totally secular people. The influence of Feng Shui has spread over much of Southeast Asia and Japan. It is especially prominent in Japan where it is used in almost every aspect of the culture, including the design of rock gardens, floral arrangements, and even food presentation. In the tradition of Feng Shui, the current advertising campaign for Mazda cars has the refrain: "It just feels right."

Ancient Chinese scholars observed that cold dry winds blow out of the north, while warm winds and rain come from the south. Life-giving water is important for any human habitation. Consequently, a house on the southern exposure of a hill is considered most auspicious. Conversely, trees and a sloping hill on the north side of the house are considered quite favorable. Western architects are now catching up with the wisdom of these ideas with passive solar architecture.

For thousands of years, colors have had great symbolic importance to the Chinese, in day-to-day life and in our architecture. Red is used lavishly in Chinatown because it is considered the color of happiness and vitality.

Brides wear it at traditional weddings, and cards and happy messages of any kind are always printed on red paper. There are several different words in Chinese for red, all of them interchangeable.

Green represents life (leaves and trees) and abundance, while blue represents the color of heaven and tranquility. The ancient Chinese used one word to describe both of these colors, and apparently saw no great distinction between them. Yellow or gold represents wealth, prosperity, and power. Yellow was the imperial color of the Manchus, and fell into disfavor for a long period after the revolution in 1911. You do not see much white in Chinatown because it is a symbol of purity and is a color of mourning. So is black, although it used to be considered a lucky color associated with money. Feng Shui practitioners are careful to coordinate the color of a room with the direction it faces.

An important tool in the use of Feng Shui is the mirror, which is used to correct adverse situations or to enhance favorable ones. Mirrors also have great symbolic value. For instance, they were buried with the dead because they were considered essential for the journey in the afterlife. Mirrors are also associated with a happy married life. Often at weddings a mirror will be introduced to reflect fortunate light on the bride. Feng Shui practitioners recommend that mirrors be placed not too high and certainly not too low. Headaches will result if mirrors are too low for the tallest person in the house to see his full reflection. A mirror placed behind the cash register of a business will have the result of increasing the profit of the business. I suppose this would be especially true if it's a false mirror with security cameras.

After viewing the gate, it's a good plan to walk up **Grant Avenue** to do some shopping.

CHAPTER 5

Grant Avenue is the street that most first-time visitors to Chinatown request information about and wish to see. You should not be in a hurry on Grant Avenue because there is so much to see and do here. In addition to this famous street, Chinatown is made up of many intriguing side streets and narrow and wide alleyways. We will stay on Grant Avenue for the time being. Begin your walk up Grant from the Gateway to Chinatown, described in the last chapter.

SHOPPING ON
GRANT AVENUE

Soak in the colorful, ornate Chinese architecture through-out this community, the green pagoda-style roofs, and the *only-in-Chinatown* red, gold and green lampposts with turned up eaves, to ward off evil spirits. Many of the buildings are decorated in these favorite and auspicious Chinese colors to symbolize happiness, prosperity, and the good life.

As you walk, listen to the sounds of the community. Most of the locals speak only Chinese. They seldom venture out of the neighborhood, especially since everything is so conveniently located. Whatever they need is right here in these 24-plus square blocks.

Stroll along to window-shop for souvenirs. There are countless small and large gift shops, far too many to list or to visit on a single outing. You could browse for hours in museum-like Chinese furniture stores and jewelry shops with displays of the loveliest of gold and jade.

Street vendors on Grant Avenue in the 1800s.

The two blocks of Grant Avenue between Bush and California are a little peninsula of Chinatown and its shopping district that extends into the financial district. Often this area is not included on maps of Chinatown, and the Chinatown Gate was originally planned to be located at Grant Avenue and California Street. The stores on Grant from Bush to Sacramento were primarily Japanese curio shops before World War II.

If you are so inclined, it is easy to spend a lot of time and money shopping along this popular street. (A couple of years ago, my friends Estelle and Greg Butchek came for a visit from Springfield, Illinois. I suggested that they go on my tour and then visit the wine country and Monterey. They went on my tour but ignored the rest of my advice. They spent the rest of their week shopping in Chinatown, and sent home over two hundred pounds of merchandise.)

In recent years, preservationists have decried the proliferation of T-shirt and camera stores along Grant Avenue. There is so much history here that many are hoping that part of Chinatown will be designated as a historic district to preserve the exteriors of the buildings.

Many of the stores along Grant Avenue are open until 9 p.m. or later to cater to the needs of tourists and visitors. Admittedly, there are some pretty silly products here such as wooden snakes and wicker finger locks. But if you are looking for something beautiful for yourself or your home, you should be able to find it here. Competition is fierce along Grant Avenue, so prices are usually good. If you are contemplating a major purchase, it is *always* a good idea to shop and compare. Most merchants will not be offended by a reasonable offer for a major purchase.

A view of Grant Avenue from Broadway.

Many stores remain open in the evenings on Grant Avenue.

Let us briefly review some of the things of beauty you might want to buy in Chinatown:

Silk—

The cultivation of silk goes back to the earliest days of recorded history in China. Technically, the silkworm is the larva of a moth, or a caterpillar. Although all caterpillars produce silk fibers, the very best comes from the *Bombyx Mori*, a large white moth that makes a steady diet of white mulberry leaves. Some caterpillars produce about a thousand feet of silk in a cocoon, although only about seven hundred feet are usable. Only about 50% of the cocoons produce first-quality silk. It takes about one thousand miles of silk fiber to produce one pound of silk. Silk, the strongest of all natural fibers, is very flexible and soft.

China is still the largest producer of silk in the world. At one time silk was worth its weight in gold, although it is not nearly as expensive now, due to improved techniques in the fields and mechanization of processing. Its beauty is translated into luxurious-feeling clothing.

Jade—

The Chinese have traditionally considered jade to be the most precious of all the earth's resources. It was thought to bring good luck and health to the wearer. The Chinese also thought that it would keep a body from decaying after death, and Taoists believed that drinking powdered jade with medicinal herbs would result in immortality.

Technically speaking, there are two kinds of jade: *jadeite* and *nephrite*. Jadeite is a silicate (a salt derived from silica, a glassy mineral) of aluminum and sodium, while nephrite is a silicate of calcium and magnesium. Both minerals are white in their purest form. It is the presence of chromium that causes both minerals to turn green, the most highly prized color. The presence of iron produces a variety of colors: black, brown, blue, pale green, and yellow.

Jade continues to be a popular gift in Chinese families for memorable occasions like weddings, special birthdays, and graduations. The windows of most of the jewelry stores in Chinatown are filled with jade pieces. One favorite design is called the *pi*— a flat disk with a hole in the center that symbolizes heaven. Tradition is that the hole in the center is one fifth of the diameter of the disk. A pi was used by the emperor as a medium to consult Heaven.

There are many semi-precious stones that closely resemble jade, so be wary of bargains that may be too good to be true. Buying from a reputable dealer and getting a written guarantee that the stone is jadite or nephrite are good ideas.

PORCELAIN—

Porcelain is an advanced form of pottery, long considered by the Chinese as a major art form. The origin of pottery goes back to at least 6000 B.C. in China and reached its zenith with the introduction of porcelain. Porcelain is a hard white ceramic made from a white clay called *kaolin* and a stone called *petuntse*. Kaolin and petuntse were found near the town of Ching-Te-Chen in Kaingsi province, known as the porcelain capital of China. In fine china, the two materials are combined in equal proportions. Both are refined into a fine white powder, combined, and heated to a temperature of 1,300 to 1,500° C. Porcelain is white and translucent and produces a bell-like resonance when struck with a hard object.

The Happy Buddha. Rub his belly for good luck.

Most authorities agree that porcelain was discovered, or invented, during the ninth century. The growing popularity of tea during this period no doubt provided a great stimulus to the ceramic arts. The oldest and best surviving relics of porcelain go back to the Sung Dynasty (960–1274).

It was during the Ming Dynasty period (1368–1644) that the highly prized jade-green porcelain called celadon was first produced. The Persians and Turks valued it not only for its beauty but also because they believed that it would change color if poisonous substances were placed in it.

The secret of making porcelain was not discovered in Europe until 1707. Foreign competition in the porcelain trade was one of the many changes that brought our forefathers to America. The turmoil in China over the last half of the nineteenth century brought an end to the Imperial Court's support for the art of porcelain and many other art forms. The kilns at Ching-Te-Chen are still active, and other pottery works have been revived. Chinese scientists are conducting research to improve and reinvigorate pottery-making techniques and the industry. One can only hope they will reachieve the glory that once existed there. They have produced some of the most beautiful and valued works of art in the world.

LACQUER—

The Chinese created the art of lacquer. Lacquer comes from the sap of a sumac tree that is native to China. Sap is drawn from the tree, strained and heated to remove excess liquid. Lacquer is then applied in thin coats to wood, metal, or porcelain. Many layers must be applied for the desired surface quality and durability. The designs are carved in after the lacquer dries. Today we see the use of lacquer expanding to include decorating pottery and wooden boxes, as well as musical instruments, furniture, and even buildings.

CLOISONNÉ—

This is one art form the Chinese did not invent, but which is very popular and available in our Chinatown. The word cloisonné comes from the French word for partition, cloison. The Chinese have been practicing the art since at least the middle of the eighth century.

Cloisonné objects are made by imposing thin strips of metal over a design on an object, such as a vase, cup, or a piece of jewelry. The design is filled in with enamel and the object is exposed to high temperature, then cooled and polished to a shine.

Bamboo—

Everyone knows about China's loving relationship with the bamboo plant. We eat bamboo shoots, use bamboo to make chopsticks, and cook or reheat food in bamboo steamer baskets. There are literally hundreds of uses for bamboo. Chinese poets and painters have celebrated its beauty and grace for centuries. The Chinese consider bamboo a symbol of longevity because of its durability and vigorous growth during cold winters.

Over 1,000 species of bamboo grow throughout the world in tropic and temperate zones. Bamboo is a type of grass that ranges in size from a few inches to over 150 feet tall, and, unlike other plants, bamboo does not expand its girth as it grows. New shoots measure their full diameter when they emerge from the ground. Some types of bamboo can grow as much as four feet in one day. Bamboo plants flower at the same time all over the world, and after flowering the plants die. The seeds of the flowers produce new plants. Flowering occurs at intervals of 30 to 120 years depending on the species. In 1984 the flowering of the Arrow bamboo nearly caused the starvation of the giant pandas in China. The pandas are very finicky eaters, and they had become dependent on this species of bamboo for their food. We should be grateful for people like Wok Wiz tour guide Dorothy Quock, who works on programs to preserve the precious pandas of China and Tibet.

After looking around the shops, continue on Grant Avenue to Sacramento Street. Cross the street to the northwest corner and walk uphill. The hill is a little steep here, but we are going only a short distance to the next corner. At **800 Sacramento,** you will pass the entrance to the **Gold Mountain Sagely Monastery.** The monastery has been here since 1988, and holds ceremonies at 6:30 p.m. on weekdays and at 12:30 p.m. on weekends. Occasionally you can see Buddhist monks walking down the street here dressed in brown robes.

If you are interested in Chinese music, visit **Excelsis Music** and the **Clarion Music Center** at **816 Sacramento**

Street for an interesting collection of Chinese musical instruments.

Traditional Chinese music is usually from a combination of string, wind, and percussion instruments. Many types of transverse bamboo flutes—the primary wind instruments of Chinese music—are on display in the shops. Brass horns make a type of sound that is noticeably absent.

The Chinese use both plucked and bowed stringed instruments. Look for the *yueqin*, or moon guitar, and the *erhu*, a two-stringed fiddle that uses a snake skin for its sounding board. Perhaps the most unusual sounds in Chinese music come from the zithers and hammer dulcimers. Also on display are percussion instruments such as gongs, cymbals, and drums.

Chinese operas were once a popular form of entertainment in Chinatown, starting at the height of the Gold Rush. Over the years, no less than seven Chinese opera houses flourished. Tour leader Martha Mew recalls that one of her fondest childhood memories is of accompanying her parents to Chinese operas in the 1930s. All that remains of the opera houses today are two movie theaters on Jackson Street.

Stores at various locations in Chinatown sell cassette tapes of traditional Chinese music, which you can hear as you walk along the streets. Chinese versions of rock and roll and other forms of music are also available throughout the area.

From this location, continue uphill toward **Waverly Place,** one of the most scenic streets in Chinatown, which will be the focus of the next chapter.

CHAPTER **6**

WAVERLY PLACE/ RELIGION

We pause at the corner of Sacramento and Waverly Place before walking down the east side of the street. The **Chinatown YMCA** is at **855 Sacramento.** Organized in 1911 to provide recreational and educational programs for the young men of the community, the YMCA is still active today. Wok Wiz tour leader George Mew recounts that he was once thrilled to win a swimming pool pass here because he was able to define the word "initiative." Being able to use the swimming pool meant that he could take a shower, a luxury, because there were no bathing facilities in his home down the street.

Waverly Place is a very picturesque street. Often called the "street of painted balconies," it reminds many visitors of the French Quarter in New Orleans. Waverly Place was known as "15 Cent Street" because that was the price of getting a haircut here in the old days, and there are still quite a few barber and beauty shops along this street. Before the Chinese revolution in 1911, Chinese men had to wear queues, or braided hair. This practice was imposed on them by the horse-loving Manchu rulers. Queues were a sign of subjugation, and it was considered treasonous to not have one. Losing one's queue meant that a man could no longer return to China. Each barber shop had a red-and- green stand with a basin on it outside as a sign of its trade. The haircuts were more like shaves, as the hairlines were shaved back an inch or more. Most Chinese wanted to be "highbrows." Working men often kept their queue coiled around their heads under a hat.

Many people are curious about the practice of religion in Chinatown. Christianity is the most widely practiced religion in Chinatown. The only Caucasian groups who supported the Chinese were Christian churches. Missionaries opened churches to gain a foothold in Chinatown as a first step toward converting the masses in China to Christianity. During the 1800s, Chinese were generally excluded from public schools here. There was a great thirst for education among the Chinese, particularly to learn to speak English. Christian churches filled this need through English-language classes. William Spear of the Chinese Presbyterian Church published a Chinese-language newspaper in 1855, which set off a long journalistic tradition in Chinatown. Today, the main Chinese newspapers in San Francisco are *Chinese World, Chinese Times,* and *Young China. Asian Week* is a popular bilingual newspaper. There is also Chinese-language radio and TV in the Bay Area; tune to Channel 26 for a sample of the television. The Chinese Television Co. at 2 Waverly Place produces programing in both the Cantonese and Mandarin languages. Another company that produces for radio and television is **Sinocast,** with a studio on Waverly Place.

My parents still read Chinese newspapers and watch Cantonese television programing for the most part. Most of their friends, and many of the over 300,000 Chinese in the Bay Area, prefer to watch programs in their native tongue.

The **First Chinese Baptist Church** across the street at **15 Waverly Place** provides a good example of the role of Christianity in the community. The church was founded in 1880 by Dr. John Hartwell, a former missionary to China. The congregation initially had nine members, and met in rented quarters by Portsmouth Square. The church organized programs for women and children, and taught many young men to speak English. The building was destroyed in the 1906 earthquake but was reconstructed and completed in 1908. Its red clinker-built brick construction creates some interesting shadows in the afternoon. The church continues to provide special programs for immigrant children and adults.

Waverly Place is the home of several district and family associations. Traditionally these organizations provided temples on the top floor of their headquarters. As you stroll down Waverly, you will probably smell incense burning from a temple. We will elaborate on associations in the next chapter.

One casualty of the revolution in 1911 was traditional Chinese religion. Many religious leaders were accused of being pro-monarchist, and many temples were closed throughout America. Since 1965 and the wave of new immigrants, there has been a great revival of traditional Chinese religion here. Chinese people practice a combination of Buddhism, Taoism, and Confucianism. The average Chinese sees no conflict in practicing more than one religious belief. As a woman on our tour put it: "It's the gambler's instinct to cover your bets." A positive side of this is that the Chinese have tended to be far more tolerant of different faiths than people elsewhere, including Europe and the United States, with their long histories of religious wars and religious discrimination.

In many ways, Chinese religions are more like philosophies than Western religions. For example, there are no regular church services. Consequently, the temples are quite small compared to Western churches. People usually attend temples around religious holidays, or to honor their ancestors, or when some earthly blessing would be appreciated. Since the temples are small and people may be there worshiping at any given time, I feel that it is intrusive to bring our groups to temples. However, some do welcome visitors and a donation of a dollar or so per person is always appreciated. You should always ask permission to take pictures; some temples do not allow it.

The Chinese have many gods and goddesses, and countless superstitions. At the same time, we are one of the most secular of all peoples. The answer to this contradiction lies in the reverence we have for our philosophers. For centuries, governmental officials and administrators were chosen for their ability to memorize and understand the classics of Chinese philosophy. There is a philosophical foundation to Chinese art, architecture, food, medicine, and religion. A basic knowledge of philosophy helps enormously in understanding the character of our people.

Confucius, Taoism, and Buddhism

One of the pillars of Chinese philosophy is the writing of Lao Tzu, perhaps more of a legendary figure than a historical personage. Some scholars believe that he was a composite figure of several sages. The name Lao Tzu means "old master." However, the consensus is that he was born in Honan in the year 604 B.C. Lao Tzu was an older contemporary of Confucius and was the curator of the Royal Library in Chou, China.

Lao Tzu lived in a time of great turmoil, violence, and corruption. Fed up with the complexities of urban life, he retired to the western frontier of China to write a book in two parts on *Tao* and *Te,* or The Book of the Way and of Virtue. The book is widely regarded as one of the most interesting in the history of thought.

Taoism, the philosophy, teaches that a cosmic law governs the operation of the universe. By living in harmony with the laws of the universe, man is able to achieve true wisdom and enlightenment. The principle means of following the Tao (meaning "the way") is to not try to force things to meet your desires and expectations. The wise man learns from the example of water and flows around obstacles. Taoism teaches that everything is in a constant state of change. Rigid attachment to anything, especially ideas, results in death, while flexibility results in renewal.

Another fundamental idea of Taoism is that all change occurs in cycles. The classic Chinese text, the *I Ching* is an analysis of the cyclic nature of change. The legend is that it was written in prison by one of the founders of the Chou Dynasty, Wen Wang, in 1133 B.C. The *I Ching* is an analysis of 64 stages of change and it is used as a manual for divination. Confucius, who edited the book, described it as the greatest of all writing and wished that he had 50 years to study it.

The concept of *Yin* and *Yang* is fundamental to Taoist thought. Essentially, Yin represents the forces of nature that accumulate and conserve, while Yang represents the forces of nature that expand or radiate. It originated with eight trigrams introduced by the legendary emperor Fu Hsi. Trigrams consist of three lines, some of them broken to represent the principle of Yin, and some of them continuous to represent Yang. In the *I Ching*, Wen Wang doubled the number of strokes, creating 64 possible combinations of continuous and broken lines. Each combination represents some law of nature. Taoists see all life as a combination of opposing or balanced forces.

Taoists believe that there are five elemental energies: water, wood, fire, metal, and earth. These energies roughly correspond to the seasons with the exception of earth which represents a balance or pivotal point between the other energies. Water, like winter, represents the extreme Yin condition in which energy is stored and accumulated. Wood, like spring, represents expansive growth and renewal. Fire, like summer, represents a period of less expansive, but more sustainable growth. Metal, like autumn, represents a period in which energy is drawn inward and conserved.

Modern science verifies what Chinese mystics have taught for centuries: our world is made of countervailing energy with pulses and rhythms. This applies not only to our biological makeup but also to our behavior. The Taoist belief is that failure is as important as success. We should look on our setbacks as opportunites to learn and grow. Rather than following the rigid rules of society and religion, Taoist believe that enlightenment comes from an awareness of the cycles of the universe.

The other pillar of Chinese philosophy was Confucius (551–479 B.C., but these dates are not certain). Confucius never knew his father, who died at age 70. The infant

Confucius was brought up in an impoverished environment by his young mother. With no formal education, Confucius was self-taught, becoming a teacher at age 23 and moving on to become a legend.

In the course of his teachings, Confucius expressed the belief that social harmony depended on people realizing their roles. He expounded an idealistic plan of five relationships to ensure unity in the family as well as in the country: ruler to subject; husband to wife; father to son; elder brother to younger brother; friend to friend. The function of the eldest male in the family is to be at the head of the hierarchy because of his wisdom attained through his life's experiences.

On a larger scale, Confucius believed that relationships between the emperor and his subjects were similar to those in the home, with the emperor ruling as a father of a large family. An ethical government where the leader set good examples and where his subjects understood their roles would result in a world of peace and tranquility.

Over a period of almost 50 years, Confucius was said to have taught more than 3,000 students. His lessons covered traditional ceremonies, archery, chariot driving, mathematics, music, and writing.

Confucius taught his students to revere learning, sincerity, and order. After his death, his influence continued to spread to Japan and Southeast Asia through his followers. His philosophy served as an integral part of Chinese thought and morality for over 2,000 years and is still very important to the Chinese. Many Chinese have strongly challenged and rejected aspects of Confucianism which seem outmoded, such as its patriarchal, undemocratic injunctions and its treatment of women as subservient. But much of value remains in the ideas.

Confucius died an unhappy man, not realizing his dream to persuade the rulers of China to eliminate abuses of power and corruption, and to pursue peace and lower taxes.

Over the course of history, the rationality of our sages was not enough to satisfy the needs of the common people. Faced with a world of hardship and forces beyond control, the Chinese looked for outside help from the gods.

It is important to make a distinction between Taoism, the philosophy, and Taoism, the religion. Taoists as religious practitioners began a search for magic potions that would confer immortality. This laid the foundation for Chinese medicine, which we will discuss at length in Chapter 9. Taoists also developed systems of meditation and physical exercise for spiritual insight and physical well-being.

The religion's founder was Chang Tao-Ling, who was born in A.D. 35 He claimed that Lao Tzu descended from Heaven to teach him his principles. Chang Tao-Ling concocted a potion that he claimed would cure many ills, and thousands flocked to him for treatment. His fee was five bushels of rice which led to his being dubbed "the rice thief." Those not cured by him were told that their faith was insufficient. One of Chang Tao-Ling's potions that was supposed to confer immortality on the emperors contained poisonous arsenic and caused a few deaths. Chang Tao-Ling lived to age 122. He is usually depicted as an old man riding a tiger.

Taoism incorporated many beliefs from Chinese folk religion, such as animism—the belief that everything, animate or inanimate, has a spirit. The Taoists worship many gods. The religion includes a concept of hell, although it is a temporary one, more like purgatory in Catholicism. The Taoists have a living head of religion who is descended from Chang Tao-Ling. Their Taoist priests, who can be married or celibate, do not proselytize, although most will give explanations of it if requested.

Buddhism was introduced into China after the fall of the Han dynasty in A.D. 221. It provided a pantheon of new gods and goddesses to comfort the people. Buddhism brought a new concept of life after death to the Chinese. Its followers believed in nirvana, an escape from the cycle of reincarnation. Over the centuries, both Buddhism and Taosim borrowed from each other, and many of the distinctions are now blurred.

GODS AND GODDESSES

Many traditional Chinese worship gods, goddesses, and their ancestors on a daily basis. There are so many popular gods and goddesses that it would take another book to cover them all. We will introduce you to a few of them.

One of my favorite gods is, not surprisingly, the Kitchen God. This tiny statue of a god resides in the kitchen by the stove throughout the year. Although there is no general agreement regarding his identity and origin, he is worshiped by both Buddhists and Taoists. He is worshiped and burned at the end of the year when he returns to Heaven to report on the family's good and bad deeds. A replacement Kitchen God assumes his duties for the new year. I hope he presides over my dinner parties.

The Tien Hau Temple on Waverly Place.

Kuan Yin is the Goddess of Mercy, the symbol of love, tenderness, forgiveness, and pity. Kuan Yin is very popular in Chinatown because we see statues of her throughout shops and businesses here. Kuan Yin represents kindness and tenderness toward mankind.

Tien Hau is a busy goddess, known as the Goddess of Heaven and Sea. She also watches over and protects travelers, writers, actors, sailors, and prostitutes. According to legend, she was a courageous woman of great strength, who fought against evil and human suffering.

There is a **Tien Hau Temple** at **125 Waverly Place,** the oldest Chinese temple in the United States.

A tradition that has returned to Chinatown in recent years is that most stores have an altar for the God of Wealth, who presides over their business. The God of Wealth is pictured as a man under a money tree with leaves of gold and silver. At the end of the year, the picture of the God of Wealth is removed and burned so that he can enter the spirit world, while a new picture signifies that the god will resume his duties for the new year. Stop in and visit the Ng family's **Ocean Trading Co.** at **117 Waverly Place.** On one side of the store there is a huge assortment of religious supplies, joss papers, incense, paper clothes, and paper money.

On the corner of Waverly and Clay, cross Waverly, walk up Clay and make a left into Spofford Alley.

CHAPTER 7

SPOFFORD ALLEY & ASSOCIATIONS

The **Chinese Free Masonry** at **36 Spofford** was a secret society and published the *Chinese Free Press,* which Dr. Sun Yat-sen used to espouse his political beliefs. After the revolutionary victory in 1911, the new government in China raised over $2 million in bond sales at this location. The **Chinese Laundry Association** at **33 Spofford** is still active. It once had a rule that each laundry had to be at least ten doors from another to reduce competition. Although the Chinese had trade guilds for centuries, many in the U.S. labor movement viewed these associations as a plot to hold down wages.

On almost any afternoon, you can hear children playing in the schoolyard behind **St. Mary's Center** on Spofford. It is here that the adorable little girls of the St. Mary's marching band practice most Saturday mornings. This band performs in the annual Chinese New Year parade and at other special functions. A slightly different sound comes from many of the buildings that line this alley. The clicking of mah jong tiles is commonly heard in the afternoons. Yes, the Chinese people love to gamble! There are several buildings that have staircases going down to businesses and social clubs.

Spofford Alley houses family associations and social clubs.

Among the most attractive and impressive buildings in Chinatown are the homes of family and district associations. Casual visitors sometimes incorrectly assume that they are savings and loan institutions.

Walk out of Spofford Alley to Clay Street, make a right turn, go up Clay Street to Stockton Street and make a left, stopping in front of the home of the **Chinese Consolidated Benevolent Association** also called **Chinese Six Companies** at **843 Stockton Street** and the **Kong Chow Benevolent Association** at **855 Stockton Street.**

The most powerful influences in Chinese culture are devotion to family life and to the land from which you came. Many historians agree that ancestral worship was a part of folk religion in China that predates recorded history. The concept of filial piety, or duty to family, was codified by Confucius 2,500 years ago and has been accepted by over 70 generations of Chinese. Providing for the spirits of departed ancestors is considered essential for maintaining the well-being of the living. The family unit is also the primary unit of social control in Chinese culture. This is particularly true of Cantonese people, who are generally considered to be the most clannish of all Chinese.

We are very deeply rooted to the land of our ancestors. Whenever strangers of Chinese ancestry meet, they first exchange surnames. The next logical question is: "Where are you from?" Although you may have never been there, or are several generations removed, the correct answer to this question is your native village in China. When asked where I live by older generation Chinese acquaintances or business associates, I don't answer "Pacifica, California," but "Hoy Ping, Canton." Sometimes my deep-rooted fourth dialect Cantonese is a telltale sign of my family's origin.

When my husband Bernie first started working with me in the office to book guests for our walking tours, he found it odd that I always wanted to know where they were from. He has since learned to adapt to this cultural remnant, so don't be surprised when we ask "where are you from?"

A recent edition of the San Francisco phone book lists 7 district, 36 benevolent, and 52 family associations. Thomas Payne's quotation "Either we hang together, or most assuredly we'll hang separately," has been literally true for the Chinese for much of their history in America.

In 1850 the first Chinese organization sponsored the participation of the Chinese at the Welcoming Ceremony at Portsmouth Square and at the funeral procession for Zachary Taylor, facts commemorated on the plaque by the stairs at Portsmouth Square.

The early Chinese

The Chinese Consolidated Benevolent Association, also known as The Six Companies, on Stockton Street.

merchants who started small businesses were in many instances small family units. New arrivals were met by family representatives and interpreters who provided them with food, lodging, and employment. Throughout most of its history, various occupations in Chinatown were dominated by people with the same surname.

These family businesses provided the foundation for the first family associations. As the name implies, family associations include all people who have a common surname and relatives remotely related by blood or marriage. In China, it is considered incestuous for people with the same surname to marry no matter how distantly they may be related. The family associations expanded to become what are known as " kinship associations," with members from different villages and districts.

Associations provided the only form of social control within the Chinese community. Because many Chinese did not believe in Christianity, they were forbidden to testify in U.S. courts, under the theory that their oaths would be meaningless. Most Chinese did not bother to learn English, and white juries and courts were unsympathetic. Associations had to arbitrate disputes between members, and rewarded those who brought to justice outsiders who harmed members. These rewards included support for the avenger's family in China if death or imprisonment were a result of the work. The rewards were attractive enough that some uninvolved third parties volunteered to "pay" for these crimes.

Because San Francisco was the central point of entry to the United States, associations gained great power over the lives of all Chinese in the United States. Associations also played a role in resolving outstanding debts for those who returned to China. This was no coincidence because associations often provided passage for the debtors' journey to America under the credit ticket system. The associations levied a fee of up to $20 to issue an exit permit to those who left America. The steamship lines agreed not to sell tickets to anyone who did not have an exit permit. Associations had representatives at the docks to collect the permits from departing Chinese. This arrangement between the associations and steamship lines continued well into the twentieth century.

In 1851, the first district associations formed in San Francisco were known as meeting halls. District associations existed in China for hundreds of years, originally consisting of groups of traveling merchants and craftsmen who joined to promote their economic interests and to provide charitable and social benefits to their members. Because of the immobility of Chinese society, considerable differences in the dialects and customs existed in areas as small as Guandong province. It was natural for people with a common heritage to want to associate with each other. These associations were generally controlled by the most literate and affluent merchants in the community.

Family associations formed power blocks within the district associations. The number of family and district associations fragmented and expanded rapidly from the time of the Gold Rush to the Exclusion Act of 1882. Early in the 1850s, a committee of association presidents was formed to represent the community at large. The purpose was to resolve disputes peacefully among associations, to entertain political dignitaries from China, and to represent the business and political interests of Chinatown to the outside world. This committee evolved over the next two decades to become The Chinese Consolidated Benevolent Association, or Six Companies as it has been known for most of its history. The Six Companies was officially founded on November 19, 1882, and incorporated under the laws of California in 1901.

The Six Companies operated much like a Court of Appeals in the U.S. judicial system to resolve disputes between businesses and associations. It served as a witness to the signing of contracts between businesses. Its attorneys vigorously fought discriminatory laws in San Francisco, in the rest of the United States, and in Canada and Mexico. For many years it served as the primary spokesman for the Chinese government in the U.S. Its current headquarters was built after the earthquake in 1906 with relief money from the Manchu government.

Due to its many political and legal victories, the Six Companies lost some of its influence because Chinese now have access to the U.S. legal system. Today, most of its energy is devoted to charitable and educational activities in the Chinatown community. However, it is still capable of doing political battle. The Six Companies recently led many

Chinatown businesses to resist the city of San Francisco's efforts to tear down the Embarcadero Freeway, damaged during the October 17, 1989, earthquake. It was an unsuccessful though valiant attempt. The Kong Chow District Association is the oldest in Chinatown; it began in 1849. The impressive temple on the top floor can be reached by elevator. It has been at this location since 1977. The original temple was built in 1857 on Pine Street.

Another function of associations was to provide cemetery plots and burial expenses for the poor. The Chinese believed that the souls of the dead would wander endlessly if their bones were not returned to their ancestral burial grounds in China. For reasons of sanitation, the bodies were buried for about six months. By then, decomposition was usually complete. The bones were then scraped clean and returned to China for their permanent burial. Associations also provided medical services and free passage for the elderly and ill who wanted to return to China.

The associations were administered by merchants and elders who had their family honor at stake. Associations frequently accumulated large sums of money from their activities as labor brokers, and from membership fees. For the most part, they operated on the honor system in terms of accountability for the money. Needless to say, abuses and power struggles often occurred.

During the 1880s, the Qing government in China took an interest in ending the corruption in associations and began recruiting scholars to serve as association presidents. In 1887, government officials decreed that presidents-elect be approved by the governor of their district in China. This in effect turned the associations into part of the diplomatic core of China. In fact, the president of an association and one assistant were given diplomatic passports, a practice that continued until 1925. By elevating association leadership above petty local interests, the intervention of the Qing government did much to prevent the financial abuses that plagued the associations.

Regional differences and prejudices persisted in Chinatown well into the 20th century. The Chinese had no true national identity until the revolution in 1911. Some violent factions traced their origins back to the overthrow of the

Ming dynasty in 1644. Because Chinatown was threatened internally by strife and greed and externally by bands of marauding whites, it is little wonder that Chinatown was such a violent place for much of its history. The vices created by the bachelor society that grew from the Exclusion Act of 1882 led to many abuses.

Although much romanticized in movies and literature, visitors should realize that the last true tong war occurred in the early 1930s. Once family life became established in Chinatown, it was no longer fashionable to settle your own scores. The Chinese detest crime and violence as much as anybody.

San Francisco has one of the lowest crime rates of any major city in America, and today's Chinatown has one of the lowest crime rates of any of the neighborhoods in the city. One reason for this is the crowds of people on the streets throughout the day and night. Visitors know that crime and violence exist everywhere in America, and it pays to be careful. But there is no reason for fear to keep anyone from visiting so fascinating an area as Chinatown.

If you do not mind walking uphill for a few minutes from the corner of Clay and Stockton, walk south one block to Sacramento Street. Make a right turn to the **Cameron House,** at **920 Sacramento.**

Donaldina Cameron (1869–1968) was a positive force for Asians, helping young Chinese slave girls to escape from their Chinese tong masters. Prostitution was a part of traditional Chinese culture because of arranged marriages and the poverty which forced young women into prostitution. The daughter became a part of the husband's family upon marriage.

Over the years, Donaldina gained the respect of the Chinese community. My father was a cook for Cameron House in 1940 on special occasions and befriended Donaldina Cameron. As a return favor, Donaldina personally escorted my mother off of Angel Island to meet my father.

In the early 1900s and into the 1960s, the Cameron House was a popular social center for the youth of Chinatown. Arts and crafts programs were organized and high-school students looked forward to parties and dances. The Cameron House was the "in place" for Chinese youth for many years, although the YWCA was close by and offered similar activities.

Today, Cameron House continues to be a youth center but also offers expanded social services to immigrants. Social workers are available to give psychological help for battered women, and there are spiritual programs such as Bible study. A book about Donaldina Cameron, *Chinatown's Angry Angel*, will interest those wanting to learn more about her contribution to and importance in Chinatown.

Walk north on Joice Street to take a look at the YWCA at **965–79 Clay Street.** The building was designed in 1930 by the great architect Julia Morgan, who created some of the most outstanding structures in California. The **YWCA** has been serving the community with programs for women since 1916.

Across the street you will see **The Commodore Stockton School** at **916 Clay Street.** The school has been here since 1915. The city originally called it "The Oriental School" because all Asians were to attend it. Today, only about 40% of the more than 800 students are Chinese because of desegregation laws.

When you are finished, return to Stockton Street, make a left turn and walk to Washington Street. Cross Washington Street and make a right turn to pause at **Old Chinatown Lane.** We will cover the activities of Old Chinatown Lane and **Ross Alley** in the next chapter.

The home of the Fong family association on Grant Avenue.

CHAPTER 8

金
山

The Chinese were confined to Chinatown after the earthquake in 1906. They took advantage of the alleys and side streets to build storefronts, and many people shared residences upstairs. Here are two alleys that have added to a most unique maze for visitors to explore.

OLD CHINATOWN LANE & ROSS ALLEY

Old Chinatown Lane houses two family associations, a beauty shop, a pet-bird store, herbal shops, and the backs of restaurants. Garment factories are plentiful in most of the alleys and back streets of Chinatown, including this one. It was a common practice for pre-school–age children to go to work with their mothers, and it was not an uncommon sight to see a three- or four-year-old child using scissors to trim off thread ends of Levi Strauss jeans. The mother's pay was 10 cents a dozen. The woman with the sewing machine closest to the door would scream *"bock guey loy lah,"* which translates to "white men coming." These men may have been Levi Strauss personnel, or labor relations people who heard that children were working illegally. The children, upon hearing this warning, were shuffled into the bathroom until the coast was clear. Today we are fortunate to have babysitters and child-care programs.

A special door at the end of this lane led to a secret passageway for the Chinese to use to hide from the police. It was a means to get from one alley to another in a quick fashion, and led to Ross Alley.

Ross Alley

Walk out of Old Chinatown Lane to get back on Washington and make a left into Ross Alley.

Back in the 1800s, Ross Alley was brimming with gambling halls and pawn shops, replaced today with a string of small garment shops and a Chinese florist. The **Sam Bo Trading Company** at **14 Ross Alley** sells Chinese religious goods, plaques, incense, lanterns, and other

The author with a happy tour group in Ross Alley.

artifacts; and there is a Chinese laundry and a one-seat barber shop at 32 Ross Alley.

The **Yau Kung Moon** kung fu studio at **37 Ross Alley** was once a favorite local hangout—the Rickshaw bar—frequented by such famous stars as Don "Tiny Bubbles" Ho and Frank Sinatra. The hostess there, Mai Tai Sing, went on to become a very famous actress. According to former Rickshaw bartender Bob Lee, the Beatles dropped in for drinks one night after their first concert in the Bay Area in 1964, sneaking in via the private passageway between Old Chinatown Lane and Ross Alley.

The Rickshaw was owned by the Lew family and was converted to this kung fu studio in 1975. Children come from all walks of life to practice kung fu on weekends, and it is a casual social club for the Lew clan during the week when the children are in school. The Yau Kung Moon studio lion dance team is very popular and is busiest during Chinese holidays and festivals. The lion dance team is made up of children and teenagers who have been practicing at the studio for years. You will recognize them by their bright yellow uniforms. It is here that the students learn about Chinese tradition, culture, discipline, and responsibility while exercising at the same time. The studio is not open to the public, but the drum beating during practice adds some color to this already attractive alley. If you happen by at the right time, you will hear them.

This is the alley where the popular **Golden Gate Fortune Cookie Factory** beckons at **56 Ross** with the aroma of freshly made cookies. An interesting tidbit: fortune cookies were first introduced in San Francisco at the Japanese Tea Garden in Golden Gate Park. The inventor did not patent the product, and the Chinese restaurateurs quickly borrowed the idea. Today fortune cookies are shipped to places all over the world, including China.

Fortune cookies are not as easy to make as it appears. The public is welcome to watch as Nancy or one of the other employees sits at the cookie machine, quickly pulls a cookie off the hot press, tucks a fortune in, and shapes it into a fortune cookie—all in a matter of seconds. This has to be done quickly or the cookie will cool and harden prematurely. The owner and manager, Frank, is usually there mixing batter, making cookies, or chatting with customers. They are generous in offering samples to all who come into their shop. In addition to fortune cookies, this small factory sells almond cookies, sesame cookies, and small or large flat cookies, all at wholesale prices.

Next door to 56 Ross is 24 Ross, a small garment factory. On the other side of 56 Ross is 32 Ross, a one-seat barber shop. The addresses have no continuity here because if the Chinese did not like their numbers, they simply changed them. Ross is a short alley, so how lost can you get? Pity, however, the mailman on the first day on the job delivering mail here. Most of his customers had the surname of Wong or Lee, so he might have gone to the Wong address instead of the Lee's.

Shirley Fong-Torres attempts to make a fortune cookie.

Numbers play a crucial role in many Chinese families. Wedding dates are picked especially to add good luck and prosperity to the marriage. Homes are purchased according to the address. To draw attention to Asians, one of my friends specifically made his asking price $288,888.88. Apparently he really wanted to sell his home. The number 8 is considered the luckiest number of all because the word *prosperity* in Chinese is synonymous with the word for eight. The number 2 stands for abundance or easy-going; the number 3 stands for life; and the number 9 stands for long life.

As you leave Ross Alley you will notice several **Chinese herbal shops** as you turn right on **Jackson.** We will learn more about Chinese medicine in the next chapter.

CHAPTER 9

There are several Chinese herbal shops on Jackson Street near the end of Ross Alley. We stop in one of them to introduce our guests to Chinese herbal medicine. Products from these shops are credited with helping maintain health and vigor, especially among the elderly. As you observe Chinatown residents, it is almost impossible not to notice the large number of elderly Chinese walking around, going about their daily business. Most of these Chinese senior citizens have clear eyes and skin, which they attribute to years of consuming Chinese soups composed of various roots, herbs, and bones. These items are available in over 15 active herbal shops in Chinatown.

CHINESE MEDICINE

You can spot an herbal shop by two key elements: 1) its aroma and 2) the sight of entire walls filled with hundreds of drawers containing the herbs. The herbalist who runs the shop is often teamed up with a doctor of traditional Chinese medicine who has an office in the back of the herbal shop.

Peek in, and often the herbalist can be seen chatting with the patient as he carefully weighs the contents of a prescription on an old balance scale. Combinations from hundreds of roots, herbs, nuts, seeds, and dates constitute a remedy for the ailment the patient is experiencing. Herbal shops exist throughout Chinatown, and business in most of them is brisk.

We drop in to visit a Chinese herbalist to experience perhaps the most exotic side of Chinatown. An introduction to the herbalist and doctor begins with a friendly nod and "good morning." We then point out the many unusual-looking items that we seem to take for granted because we grew up surrounded by them. I still wrinkle up my nose when my mother prescribes a certain foul-tasting tea for a cold. It's fun to watch a group wrinkle up *their* noses when I suggest they try some ginseng tea or when I pass out bits of ginseng root for them to munch on. The shark's fin, contained in several large glass jars, can cost more than $100 a pound. But it's worth its weight in gold, explains Mr. Lim, the herbalist. It is good for energy and power, as he demonstrates by pounding his chest with both hands and laughing heartily.

Like so many other aspects of life in Chinatown, the herbal shops have a tradition directly tied to the position of the Chinese as a minority group. The first Chinese in America had to depend heavily on themselves for medical care. They could not speak English, were excluded from white hospitals, and probably could not have afforded the medical expenses anyway. Entrusting life-and-death decisions to strangers and strange treatments required a cultural leap that was seldom made. Most early settlers brought little bags of herbal remedies with them from their homeland.

Though the Chinese were reluctant to venture to Western doctors, some very prominent Caucasians sought treatment from the Chinese. An herbalist named Li Po Ti established a very successful practice at Portsmouth Square. Lo Po Ti was well known for his ability to cure rheumatism. Two of his patients were Leland Stanford and Mark Hopkins, the railroad barons who lived on Nob Hill and who were half of California's famous Big Four. Li Po Ti amassed a fortune in real estate through earnings from his medical practice.

The basic Chinese philosophy of medicine is intriguing. Westerners generally wait to get sick and develop symptoms before consulting a doctor. The Chinese visit doctors to *stay* healthy. If a Chinese becomes ill, he or she holds the doctor personally responsible. The Chinese feel that seeing a doctor after becoming ill is like digging a well after becoming thirsty. They prefer to buy ingredients for herbal teas and soups as preventive medicine or for maintenance of good health.

Chinese medicine has philosophical roots in the Taoist

principles that all life consists of a delicate balance of opposing forces, and that most diseases are long term, systemic, and nutritionally based.

Chinese herbal shops carry over-the-counter prescriptions for minor ailments which are dispensed by the pharmacist after the client describes his or her ailment.

For more serious ailments, a patient consults a physician who will prescribe herbal medicine especially for the person. Patients are generally given a pulse diagnosis lasting several minutes. Chinese traditional medicine teaches that there are at least twelve different pulses and that the condition of each vital organ is indicated by these pulses. The doctor has the patient place a wrist on a pillow while he takes the various pulses with great concentration. A diagnosis also involves looking into the patient's eyes and at his tongue.

In the back room of the herbal shop, the Chinese doctor asks the patient questions about his daily life, some of which may seem irrelevant. His purpose is to see if the patient's system needs to be sped up or slowed down. After the examination, the doctor determines the internal imbalances of the patient, and writes a prescription to help restore the balance. The prescription is taken out to the Chinese pharmacist.

The morning after Thanksgiving, one of our guests confided to Mr. Lim that he had heartburn and a stomachache because he ate too much turkey the night before. He asked for a remedy and was prepared to pay the seven-dollar consultation fee. Mr. Lim took a good look at the man, stepped back to converse with the doctor, and came right back. His diagnosis was "don't eat so much." The rest of the group broke up in laughter, and I reminded the embarrassed man to leave the seven dollars on the counter (just kidding, of course).

A pharmacist usually dispenses remedies by using a hand balance scale to weigh several of the five to six hundred most popular medicinal items kept in the small drawers in the store. A very complete store might have as many as *three thousand* items. Prescriptions consist of an assortment of barks, berries, roots, flowers, or other animal or mineral cures that have been used for centuries.

A Chinese herbalist fills a prescription.

Often, the bill will be tabulated with an abacus, the "Chinese cash register."

The patient brews the medicine for a prescribed length of time to form a tea. A typical procedure is to heat "four rice bowls of water, add the ingredients and cook until reduced to one rice bowl of liquid. Strain and drink." Like most

 medicine, this is often bitter tasting. A small envelope of sweets, usually California raisins, is given to counteract the bitterness. When I was a little girl, I ate the raisins first and tried to pour the tea down the drain when my parents weren't watching. I was usually caught. Repeat visits are often necessary for further pulse examinations and modifications of the prescription. Many patients have personally told me that they have found relief only after visits to the herbalist.

Herbal medicine has gained respectability and is taken far more seriously than before. The state of California now licenses doctors and pharmacists for the practice of herbal medicine. In California, the public is beginning to realize that Chinese traditional medicine is a vast field, one which is based on over 5,000 years of practice. More scientists in the East and West are taking a careful look at this medical system because of the obvious effectiveness of herbs and other treatments. Further research will show

This should cure you of arthritis: a blend of roots and herbs.

not only which herbs and foods are truly effective in preventing or curing disease but also why they work.

Chinatown's flourishing herbal trade nearly disappeared during the Cold War period of the 1950s and 1960s when commerce with China was prohibited by federal law. Then in 1973, with the resumption of trade with China, the herbalist business was reborn.

INTERESTING ITEMS IN THE CHINESE HERBAL SHOP

Among the many hundreds of herbs and food cures available, here is a list of just a few that are fascinating just to take a look at. If you want to learn more, consult some of the books mentioned in the bibliography.

BIRDS' NEST—
I always imagine that some of my ancestors must have been very hungry when they first ate some of the food items in Chinatown. Why else would anyone contemplate eating a bird's nest? Produced by swallows that live in huge caves in the East Asian tropics, mating males and females secrete a gelatinous saliva used in nest making. The most preferred are called white nest, and they are nearly all saliva. Less valuable black nests may contain feathers, grasses, and moss. The nests are harvested and dried and must be washed several times before cooking. Believers in the virtues of bird's nests pay a fortune for this delicacy in order to have a good complexion and because it is considered nutritious. Let us move on to another topic before we need a Chinese remedy for indigestion.

BLACK FUNGUS OR CLOUDS' EARS—
Since the 16th century Chinese pharmacies have

been using black fungus and clouds' ears to render the blood fluid. Black fungus is a standard ingredient in two of my favorite dishes, *mu shu pork* and *Hot 'n Sour Soup*. It is used commonly in a traditional Chinese New Year vegetarian dish, *lo han jai*, and with scafood. Like Chinese dried mushrooms, black fungus is rehydrated by soaking in hot water for 10 minutes. After soaking, they turn a light brown and resemble ears.

CHINESE ALMONDS AND OTHER NUTS—

Available in cellophane bags, there is always a wide variety of nuts for use in soups. One health-conscious woman on our tour went on an incredible spree in the herbal shop, buying a package of each kind of nut and seed. Asked what she was going to do with her purchases, she replied that she would figure that out when she got home but reckoned all of this must somehow be good for her.

CHRYSANTHEMUM—

Bagged leaves of chrysanthemum are used for teas. Chrysanthemum tea is often requested in the dim sum houses—when you order a pot, lift the lid to look at the pretty flowers floating around.

Chrysanthemum tea is highly reputed as beneficial for vision problems. It is recommended as a treatment for pinkeye, using the leaves in an eyewash or made into a tea to drink.

DEER ANTLERS—

These are often ground for use in herbal tea to give the patient greater strength. I can only offer a bit of anecdotal evidence of antler effectiveness. When a friend of mine developed a severe rash from a food allergy while in China, her hosts took her to a Chinese hospital. The doctor rubbed deer antlers on all the affected areas, and she was just fine the next morning. Oftentimes you will see the pharmacist removing the fur from antlers when he has a spare moment; the fur is thought to be a powerful aphrodisiac. Deer antlers are exported from Ohio and Minnesota to China.

DRIED BLACK MUSHROOMS—

Chinese chefs throughout the world prefer dried *shiitake* mushrooms to the fresh ones now available in many markets. Medical texts refer to them as a "plant of immortality," and they are featured in classic Chinese dishes. Black mushrooms have brown or black caps that are usually one to three inches in diameter. The very best are thick with white fissures in the cap, and these premium mushrooms are usually sold in attractive gift boxes. They grow naturally on fallen oak or chestnut trees in winter. They are called *shiitake* mushrooms by

An herbalist carefully weighs out two doses of a prescription, and uses an ancient balance scale.

the Japanese because they grow on the *shi* tree, an oak-related species. These mushrooms can be reconstituted by soaking them in hot water for about 10 minutes. Herbal shops offer black mushrooms in bulk for between $10 and $30 per pound.

DRIED SCALLOPS—

These are a close relative of our sea scallops known as "conpoy" in English. They are very expensive and are used sparingly to flavor sauces, soups, or rice congee. Dried scallops are amber in color and are rehydrated by steaming in water or rice wine for about 20 minutes. The liquid makes an excellent addition to the sauce or soup. Often the scallops are shredded before being added to the other ingredients. Dried scallops cost between $40 and $60 per pound, depending on the quality. On very special occasions, such as a wedding, they may be served as the main ingredient in an entree. It is always a good idea to attend a traditional Chinese wedding banquet if you are invited because it is exciting to try the various exotic and symbolic dishes.

FAT CHOY OR BLACK MOSS—

This hairlike moss is gathered along China's southern coast. It certainly has no eye appeal since it looks like an old wig. It is considered an excellent source of fiber. Fat choy is used as an ingredient in *lo han jai,* the Buddhist vegetarian stew that is commonly served for Chinese New Year. *Fat choy* in Chinese means prosperity, which is one reason why lo han jai is so popular at traditional Chinese New Year dinners.

GINGKO NUTS—

I spent the better part of my childhood helping my mother break up gingko nuts with a hammer for our many herbal soups. These nuts look like tiny footballs with hard beige shells. Inside is a small pale-yellow meat that can be mashed if you hit the shell too hard. Gingko nuts are a popular remedy for bladder and urinary ailments, but are used primarily in soups and claypot stews and sometimes in dim sum as an addition to the filling for stuffed lotus or bamboo leaves.

GINSENG—

This is considered a premier medicinal herb by millions
of people. The ancient Chinese medical text from 200 B.C., *Shen Nong Herbal,* claims that ginseng vitalizes the internal organs, calms nerves, improves vision and intellect, and prolongs youth by making one feel healthy and young.

Millions of Asians still agree with the old herb master and spend a fortune on ginseng roots and tea throughout the world. (Native Americans in much of North America also use ginseng as a medicinal herb.)

Ginseng roots can be used in preparing herbal soups and other dishes, or ground into pill form or for tea powder. Ginseng is a short perennial shrub that grows in shaded hardwood forests in Asia and North America. The largest resource for wild and cultivated ginseng in the United States is now in central Wisconsin.

LILY STEMS—

Pale brown and about three inches long, these "golden needles" are dried unopened flowers of yellow and orange day lilies. Medicinally, they are used for mild pain relief. Legend has it that pregnant Chinese women used to wear lily stems around their waists in hopes of producing a baby boy. Lily stems are used most commonly when steaming food and as an addition to many stir-fried dishes.

RED DATES—

These are imported from China and are used to add sweetness to soups, and also in a variety of steamed dishes, such as with chicken and black mushrooms. These little dried jujubes are bright red and are used as an antidote to the bitterness of many Chinese herbal remedies. The red color is auspicious and brings good fortune.

SEA SLUGS—

For centuries the Chinese have pursued these shell-less creatures from the coast of Africa to the South Seas and Australia. Recently, sea slugs have become so scarce that prices have soared in China. They are used primarily to enhance male virility. Sea slugs are dried and must be soaked for several days before cooking. After cooking, they become spongy, translucent, and taste something like boiled pork fat. Needless to say, the taste for sea slugs has not spread much beyond Chinatown and China.

SHARK'S FIN—

Shark's fin soup has long been considered one of the most exotic and expensive Chinese food items. It is usually purchased as pieces of hard, dried grayish fins. A side-view peek reveals the golden tendons, the part that is used for soup. There is a shop on Wentworth Alley that sells cleaned shark's fin for about $25 per pound, considered a bargain. The higher quality shark's fin can cost well over $100 per pound. When cooked, the shredded, golden-colored shark's fin represents the gold of prosperity.

TIGER BALM—

This has become popular far beyond Chinatown, and I am constantly amazed at how many of my tour guests already know about Tiger Balm. This popular ointment from Shanghai has been around for over a half century. Nowadays, it is endorsed by Joe Montana of the San Francisco '49ers, a man who knows about aches and pains. Tiger Balm comes in three sizes and two strengths: the Tiger Balm Red is extra strength; Tiger Balm White is regular strength. It gives relief for pain due to colds, flu, strains, rheumatism, simple backaches, joint pain, and muscle soreness.

WHITE FLOWER OIL—

An analgesic balm available in small-to medium-sized bottles. Gently dab a little gently on the temples or under your nose when you're not feeling well. It is used for temporary relief of minor muscular aches and pains due to fatigue, strain, and arthritis.

WHITE FUNGUS—

This resembles a dry, yellowish sponge about two inches in diameter. White fungus is a close relative of black fungus and is said to promote longevity. White fungus does not have a very distinct flavor, much like bean cake. It absorbs the flavors from other foods. It adds a soft yet crunchy texture to soups and stir-fry dishes.

After looking at herbs, continue down Jackson Street to Grant, make a right turn and find the fabulous tea shop discussed in the next chapter.

When you get to the corner, make a right turn and look for the green awning at **Ten Ren Tea Shop.**

CHAPTER 10

CHINESE TEA

We visit the largest tea emporium in San Francisco, the grand **Ten Ren Tea Shop** at **949 Grant Avenue**, to learn about Chinese tea and for a tasting. More than 50 varieties of tea are offered here, and we usually sample two or three types, and occasionally our tour groups are treated to a private tea ceremony. It is a quiet, almost spiritual time that reinvigorates us for the rest of the tour. It is a pleasure to introduce our visitors to the many tastes of tea in a very popular stop. These teas are the real thing, which you're unlikely to find in a supermarket. They come from specific growing regions and are processed in labor-intensive ways, which means they are often not available in large enough quantities for mass distribution. Imported tea-serving ceramics and other tea accoutrements are also available at Ten Ren.

An ancient story claims that tea drinking began three thousand years ago by accident when tea leaves blew into the boiling water of Shen Nong, the legendary emperor who is also credited with inventing herbal medicine and agriculture. He was quick to extoll the virtues of tea both as a refreshment and as an herbal remedy.

Many Chinese people consider tea a magical beverage that is both soothing and stimulating. Unlike most other taste treats, there are few drawbacks to tea drinking. Most teas are low in caffeine—about half as much as coffee—and science has not established any risk in the *moderate* use of caffeine. There is also some scientific evidence that substances in tea are beneficial for lowering blood pressure and cholesterol, aiding digestion, and helping to prevent tooth decay. Herbal teas have been used in China for their medicinal value for thousands of years.

In many ways, the Chinese love of tea is comparable to an appreciation of fine wine in the West. In each case, the finished product is an expression of the soil and climate where it is grown. The plants that produce tea and wine survive for many years with careful cultivation. There are many ways of processing the finished product to provide a wide variety of taste sensations. People in different regions have varying tastes for the product, some preferring blends of tea leaves (or grapes). Both wine and tea must be handled carefully to preserve their integrity. The color and aroma of each should be savored before drinking.

Tea has played a very significant role in history. The earliest reliable reference to tea goes back to the third century B.C. Historians believe that tea was first cultivated in Sichuan, and spread throughout China from there. During the Tang dynasty in the seventh and eighth centuries, tea drinking became an art, and was often surrounded with great ritual. At that time, China was the largest nation on earth. Merchants from Persia came in great caravans with jade, agate, and crystal to trade for porcelain, silk, and tea. Buddhist priests introduced tea to Japan in the ninth century. Dutch traders brought it to Europe in the early seventeenth century. As the century progressed, tea replaced coffee as the beverage of choice in many nations, especially England and Russia.

Going back to the Tang dynasty, tea has been a favorite target for taxation. Consequently, it has often been smuggled and adulterated. After Britain passed the Tea Act of 1773, American colonists did both. Resentment over taxation without representation led to the Boston Tea Party on December 3, 1773, a crucial event of the American

Revolution. The constant need for fresh tea led to the development of those graceful and gorgeous clipper ships that ruled the seas for many years in the 1800s. There was a dark side, too. Imbalances of trade in tea and other goods lead to Western intervention in China, resulting in some of the terrible conditions that caused my forefathers to come to America. It is difficult to imagine that a peaceful beverage like tea resulted in so much violence in the past.

Chinese tea ceremonies are traditionally performed on special occasions such as weddings or engagements. When a man's family presents a prospective bride with a gift of tea, it is a signal to matchmakers to stop proposing candidates. On her wedding day, the bride offers a cup of fine tea to her mother-in-law in a tea ceremony. The older woman's acceptance of the tea symbolizes her acceptance of the bride into the family. Tea ceremonies may also be performed to close a business deal or to help resolve a dispute. Increasingly they are performed routinely just to share a quiet moment with a few close friends.

A tea ceremony begins with the host pouring a couple of tablespoons of tea into a tea funnel, a small bowl with small spout on one side. The host then presents the tea to

A tea set used for a traditional tea ceremony.

the guest in much the same way that a sommelier presents a bottle of wine. The quality of the tea represents the esteem that the host has for the guest. I always tell the guests to be wary if they see a tea bag: it means you have a lot of work ahead of you.

The host next places the tea in the pot and rinses it for a few seconds with hot water. This rehydrates the tea, washes away any dust, and heats the pot. This water is then used to heat the tea pitcher and the teacups. The host may again pass around the teapot, so that the guests may enjoy the aroma of the rehydrated tea.

Proprietor of Ten Ren Tea Shop, Mrs. Lee, prepares tea for the author.

The host then adds more water and brews the tea for about 30 seconds, and pours it into the minute tea pitcher to stop the brewing process. The tea is then dispensed to the cups, a little at a time if you have a large group, so that the flavor will be uniform for all the guests. It is traditional for the guest to hold the cup with both hands, to show respect for the beverage. At this point, I propose a toast to the guests, wishing that they have lots of long noodles (representing a wish for a long life) and a memorable visit to San Francisco.

Many people are surprised by the small cups and teapots used in the tea ceremony. These small clay pots are ideal for speeding up the brewing process and creating a uniform flavor in the tea. Don't worry, because quality teas can be brewed from four to ten times from a single batch of tea leaves. Many people feel that the best flavor comes from the second brewing of the tea. You simply add about 10 seconds to the brewing time for each subsequent serving of tea; tea leaves can be reused over a 24-hour period. These tiny tea sets can be works of art and make a splendid gift or souvenir.

The Chinese have no particular time of the day to drink tea. Sharing a cup of tea is an essential step in showing respect for a companion. A host brings tea to the table before food is served so that guests may relax and let the tea aid in digestion. Most Chinese do not drink tea during the course of the meal. Green or oolong tea without milk or sugar is served at the beginning of the meal. After a meal, a strong flavored tea such as oolong may be served to cleanse the pallet. Drinking tea throughout the workday has long been common with Chinese workers. In China, they keep a thermos of hot water with them for refills. Drinking tea while socializing with friends and family at dim sum is *very* popular in southern China. In Hong Kong restaraunts it is not considered rude for patrons to stand behind other diners waiting for their seats. The diners continue to eat and drink tea, ignoring the person behind them who is invariably reading a newspaper or magazine and in no hurry.

Newcomers to Chinatown may experience a few rituals at teahouses that deserve explanation. One is the tapping of fingers or knuckles on the table after tea is poured as an expression of thanks. This practice springs from the legend that Emperor Qian Long made an incognito visit to southern China during the 18th century. To preserve his anonymity, the emperor would occasionally pour tea for his manservant and other guests. Since he could not kowtow (bow) to the emperor while Qian posed as a commoner, the servant invented the practice of tapping on the table with his knuckles to represent a kowtow.

Teapot lids are often tipped and left askew at the tea-houses as a signal to your waiter that more tea is wanted. Waiters also leave the lids askew to signify that a table is ready to be cleared. Legend has it that this practice began when a cranky customer refused to pay for his meal because a waiter removed the lid and allowed his pet bird to escape. Apparently, the customer placed his beloved bird into an empty teapot for safekeeping while he had his meal. I presume this is not a common problem, but thrifty Chinese merchants do not like to take any chances.

Tea comes from *camellia sinensis,* an evergreen tree related to the camelia bush. Although the trees can grow to 40 feet or more, commercial growers prune them to a height between two and five feet. The trees now grow in a band on both sides of the equator all around the globe. Teas grow best in mountains below 6,000 feet. The trees take three to five years to produce a crop, and can produce for as long as 40 years. The choicest leaves are the last two on the branch along with the bud. Tea is harvested from spring to fall, with the best part of the harvest coming in the spring.

Although there are countless varieties and blends of tea, there are three basic ways of processing the leaves after harvesting. The degree to which the tea leaves are fermented or oxidized determines if it will be a black tea, a semi-fermented tea like oolong, or green tea.

Of the three teas, the black tea is the most complex to make. First, the tea leaves are wilted by exposing them to the sun or other heat for about 18 hours. This makes the leaves pliable so that they can be rolled. The leaves are rolled and twisted to break down their cell walls. After the leaves are separated and sifted, the fermentation process begins. (It's called fermentation, but it's actually oxidation. No yeasts are acting on the leaves, only oxygen.) The tea leaves are spread out in a cool place for several hours. The chemicals in the leaves undergo changes that produce the flavor and color of the finished product. The processor must carefully monitor this process because more oxidation produces more color but less flavor. The tea is then fired, or dried, to stop the oxidation process and to preserve it. The tea processor is left with about one pound of finished product for every four pounds of tea leaves processed.

The processing of green tea is the simplest. Fresh-picked leaves are heated by steaming, baking, or pan-frying to sterilize them. The leaves are then rolled and dried to preserve them.

Oolong tea, also called "semifermented," is a full-bodied tea that is most often served in Chinese restaurants. Oolong leaves must be picked at the peak of their perfection and processed very quickly. They are spread out in the direct sun and are shaken several times to bruise the edges of the leaves. The bruising of the edges causes them to oxidize and yellow. Eventually, the edges become reddish while the center of the leaf remains green. At this point, the leaves are stir-fried or fired at a very high temperature to preserve them. Oolong teas keep very well because they have a very low moisture content.

A visit to Chinatown is a great opportunity to acquaint yourself with the pleasures of tea. If you have only tried the teas available at your local supermarket, you're missing a lot. Some teas that you may want to try are the following:

PU-ERH—
sold in large cakes and valued for its medicinal properties. It is known as a remedy for lowering cholesterol and providing relief from diarrhea and indigestion. Pu-erh is a semifermented tea that stores well, but its earthy, rather strong flavor is not to everyone's taste. Pu-erh is often combined with chrysanthemum blossoms to create a refreshing blend.

GUNPOWDER—
an unfermented tea that gets its name from its gray-green color and pelletlike shape. It produces a light-green tea that is fragrant and mildly bitter. Gunpowder tea was the first tea to be exported from China, and once accounted for about two-thirds of the tea imported to the United States. It contributes to strong bones and teeth because it is a good source of fluoride. Gunpowder tea is popular as an iced tea, and is not considered expensive.

OOLONG—

a semiblack tea from the mountainous region of western Fujian province in China. Its aroma is often compared to that of ripe peaches. It is a good compromise between the heavy black teas and very mild green teas, and my tea of choice.

PUOCHONG—

a subtle semiblack tea that is less fermented than oolong and often scented with gardenia and jasmine flowers. It comes from Foochow or Taiwan.

JASMINE—

a large-leaf tea scented with dried jasmine blossoms. It is often served in dim sum teahouses and also after a meal to cleanse the pallet. Called *heung peen*, its refreshing aroma makes for a popular afternoon tea. Jasmine tea is most commonly used in northern China.

KEEMOON—

the cabernet sauvignon of teas. It is a dark black tea with a rich aroma that many experts consider the best of China's black teas. And like that noble wine, its quality varies from year to year. Keemoon has a spicy smoothness that goes well with most food.

LAPSANG-SOUCHONG—

a full-bodied black tea that comes from Hunan, Fukien, and Taiwan. Its distinctive sweet, smoky aroma and taste make it an excellent after-dinner tea.

LICHEE BLACK TEA—

treated with the juice of lichee fruit to make a delightful, tangy, and unusual treat. I like it hot or cold, and some adventurous gourmets claim that it combines especially well with ice cream.

ROSELLE TEA—

a blend of black tea and hibiscus flowers, the Ten Ren Tea Shop serves this regularly to visitors as a sample. It is an herbal tea, naturally sweet, and is popular hot or iced.

Tea should be stored in a cool, dark area in tight containers to prevent loss of flavor and absorption of unpleasant flavors. Black teas retain their freshness the longest; green teas are the most perishable. The beautiful airtight tea containers sold throughout Chinatown are a decorative and functional way to preserve the freshness of your tea. Stored in one of these containers, tea will last up to two years.

There must be nearly as many theories about how to make a good cup of tea as there are tea drinkers. The following works for me:

1. Unless you have large parties, stick to a small pot. Too much volume will often cause the leaves to stew and diminish the flavor. Large pots also slow down the brewing process. Choose a pot that is comfortable to your hand and one that has a lid that won't fall off when you pour the tea.

2. Choose a good quality tea. Quality tea tastes better and last longer. A pound of good tea will yield about a hundred cups, so tea is an inexpensive beverage even if you use the very best. Prices range from $7 per pound to well over $100 per pound.

3. *Never* use hot water from the tap or water that has been standing in the pipes for long. It will taste flat and may contain chemicals and off flavors from the plumbing. Some purists recommend using mineral water, although I think that's going a bit too far. However, those who have tasted tea in China from certain legendary springs insist that the water is a crucial factor, and that the experience is unforgettable. So if you're on an ultra-serious quest for the ultimate tea, you really may want to experiment with various bottled waters.

4. Heat the pot with hot water before brewing the tea. This rinses the pot and will keep the tea hot longer after it is brewed.

5. Use one teaspoon of loose tea for each cup. If you are dealing with large volumes or like your tea strong, add an extra teaspoon to the teapot.

6. Pour the water over the tea immediately after it comes to a vigorous boil. If the water boils too long, it will lose its oxygen and taste flat.

7. Brewing time varies with the type of tea, individual tastes, and the size of the teapot. One to three minutes should be sufficient for green teas, while black teas may take from three to five minutes.

8. Enjoy the color and aroma of your tea before drinking it. And, a toast: here's to your health!

Peggy Wong, hostess at Ten Ren Tea Shop, offers a toast.

A well-brewed cup of good quality tea can certainly add some beauty to your day. For even more beauty, you may want to visit **Far East Fashion** at **953 Grant,** next door to Ten Ren Tea Shop. It is a shop of linen tablecloths, silk blouses, silk jackets, coin purses, and slippers. Return to the corner of Jackson Street and Grant Avenue. Cross Grant and walk downhill to the **I Chong Art Gallery** at **661 Jackson,** and enter the world of traditional Chinese art, the topic of the next chapter.

CHAPTER 11

CHINESE BRUSH PAINTING

After leaving the Ten Ren Tea Shop, go down Grant Avenue to visit the **I Chong Art Gallery** at **661 Jackson Street.** (Some of our tour groups are personally treated to a demonstration of Chinese brush painting.) The proprietor, Mr. Y. K. Lau, his son Gary, or another artist in residence creates a beautiful painting for us within a matter of minutes.

I have known Mr. Lau ever since starting my walking tours. I met him while conducting a tour, as we strolled down Wentworth Alley. Mr. Lau greeted me and introduced himself, and we engaged in a brief conversation. He was curious about who I was, and invited us into his gallery. I politely declined that day, as my mother taught me to never speak to strangers, let alone go anywhere with them.

A few days later, Mr. Lau was in the alley again, and it was then that we learned he was the owner of the framing shop where we paused to talk about Chinese art. Again, he invited us to his studio, and now it seemed disrespectful to refuse him. His upstairs gallery displays walls full of beautiful framed silk embroidery which portray landscapes and other Chinese symbolism. Downstairs in his studio, he masterfully demonstrated Chinese brush painting. Our friendship developed from that moment forward, and came to include his family, too.

My friend has been a brush-paint artist for over 50 years, but one day, he seemed particularly nervous to me. He explained that his *master*, visiting from China, was coming to instruct him that afternoon. On my next visit, I learned that Mr. Lau's master had congratulated him on his improvement. Chinese traditional painters are never too old to learn.

Mr. Lau is an artist with heart. Once, while my tour leaders George Mew, Larry Mak, and I were walking back from an especially exhausting group tour, Mr. Lau greeted us in front of his gallery. We stopped to chat, and somehow the conversation turned to George. Mr. Lau learned that George and his wife Martha had ten grandchildren. A few weeks later, I noticed a huge painting that Mr. Lau was working on in his studio; it was of two large pandas lounging in a bamboo grove with ten smaller pandas prancing around in all directions. Mr. Lau explained that he was going to give George and Martha that painting.

PRINCIPLES OF BRUSH PAINTING

Chinese painting is based on six principles that have endured for over 1,500 years.

1. A painting should have life and vitality. Chinese paintings usually convey the Taoist admiration for the beauty of nature and the web of life. Each artist should put something of his own thought and belief into the painting. Mr. Lau's favorite paintings are whimsical pictures of animals, such as pandas munching on carrots, or cats peeking into a fish pond.

2. The brush should be used in a very controlled manner. Experts examine each stroke before considering the work as a whole. Each stroke should be executed in the traditional manner. We can be mesmerized by Mr. Lau's serenity as he carefully applies his strokes to the rice paper.

3. The subject should be recognizable. Unlike many

Western painters, traditional Chinese artists do not paint with the subject in view. They paint from their inner vision and feelings for the subject. Although the scene, colors, and light spring from the mind of the artist, the result is expected to be easily recognizable. Chinese paintings are usually confined to one subject. Mr. Lau almost always starts his paintings of animals with the animal's eyes. Oftentimes, we cannot guess what he's painting until much later. Mr. Lau quietly smiles as people begin to guess out loud.

4. Color should be used carefully. The best brush strokes are made with black on paper. Blacks and many shades of gray are viewed as positive colors. The more difficult medium of silk works best for vivid primary colors. Mr. Lau always starts with black ink, adding color later on if the painting requires it.

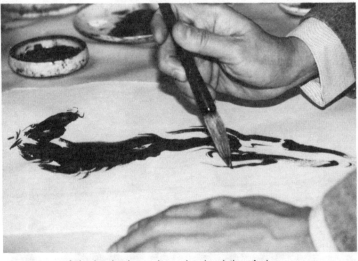

Artist Lau begins work on a brush painting of a horse.

5. The picture should be very carefully balanced. About two-thirds of the paper or silk is generally left unpainted. Space is important in many Chinese art forms, and helps to concentrate the mind and eye on the subject. More space is left above the image than below, and a similar

Artist Y. K. Lau usually begins a painting with the eyes—in this case, of a panda bear.

proportion should be used when the painting is hung on the wall. Unpainted space above the subject represents heaven, and space below represents earth. The subject matter unifies heaven and earth. Oftentimes, Mr. Lau contemplates the paper and traces with his finger the placement of the subject matter before taking brush in hand. After finishing the painting, he surveys the composition before deciding on which side to sign his name and add his personal *chop*, showing that this is a signed original. (The chop is a Chinese signature applied with a carved stamp.)

6. Practice and improvement are achieved by copying. There is no stigma of "unoriginality" attached to copying the work of masters. Practicing brush painting is very analogous to playing a musical instrument. With many centuries of tradition behind them, Chinese artists strive to build on the achievements of those who preceded them. It is inspiring to watch Mr. Lau's young students practice brush strokes under his patient guidance.

The artist always signs and dates each painting.

THE METHOD OF
BRUSH PAINTING

A brush-paint artist begins by rubbing an ink stick on an ink stone. There are many types of decorative ink stones from China; some are even made from jade. An ink stone is usually a block of nonporous slate with a flat grinding area and a rounded indentation that serves as an inkwell. Most ink sticks are black because that is the most important color in Chinese art. The main ingredient of the ink stick is pine soot, which comes from the burning of pine branches that are neither too old nor too young. The pine soot is blended with a special gum and moulded into sticks of varying sizes and shapes. Most ink sticks are decorated with calligraphy and an animal or landscape.

The artist creates ink by adding about a half teaspoon of water to the inkwell and a few drops to the ink stone. Much pressure is required to grind ink from the stick, and it takes about two hundred circular grinding motions to prepare a half teaspoon of ink. While grinding the ink, the artist composes the picture in his mind so that he and the ink will be ready simultaneously. The vigorous grinding loosens the muscles of the fingers, hand, and arm for the strokes that will follow.

When the ink has reached the right consistency and color, the artist will grasp a brush. Special Chinese brushes are required to complete the many complex strokes used in brush painting. The brushes are made with natural fiber, usually lamb's wool, goat hair, or even mouse whiskers. The fibers are always compacted very tightly so that a brush can complete several strokes with a single load of ink. Handles are usually made of bamboo because of its light weight and ability to withstand immersion in water. Many stores throughout Chinatown sell brushes.

The artist must be very careful to load the correct amount of ink on the brush, and most strokes require that the ink coats the bristles fully. Two or three colors may be loaded on the brush at once, so that tone and shades are achieved with one stroke. Brushes are held vertically to begin each stroke, with no part of the artist's hand touching the painting or table. The changing angle of the brush, the pressure, and degree of wetness of the brush all influence the result of each stroke.

It is very important that the paper be absorbent in brush painting. The colors go completely through the paper, making it very difficult to revise by painting over an image. Usually rice paper is used, although some artists use paper made from bamboo or mulberry. Since the paper is very absorbent, the artist must place paper towels or other paper under the painting to absorb the excess ink.

Artist inking the chop.

When the painting is completed, the artist will apply his or her unique chop. The act of applying a seal to paintings has been practiced for centuries, although its origins are obscure. The first seal placed by the artist documents its authenticity, and it may be followed by another that records some facet of the artist's personality. If two chops are used, they will undoubtedly have reversed colors reflecting the principle of Yin and Yang. An approving owner might apply his or her chop to the painting to

Mr. Lau with his panda bear painting.

record the ownership. Many chops are made with jade or ivory and are works of art themselves.

The red ink used with chops should not fade or run for hundreds of years, and it can be quite expensive. It is a thick red paste made from cinnabar, shredded raw silk, and oils. The seal is pressed into this ink a few times and then applied to the painting with very uniform pressure. Applying a chop is a part of the artist's ritual and gives a beautiful splash of color to the finished product. Chops can be purchased at many stores throughout China-town. We recommend **Kee Fung Ng Gallery** at **757 Grant Avenue.**

After the chop is applied, the painting must be allowed to dry for about 15 minutes. It is then glued to a firm paper with a very thin starch or wallpaper paste. It can then be matted and framed to protect its beauty. Chinese paintings are never square; they can be oblong in either direction.

The most common shape of a Chinese traditional painting is long and narrow, especially for landscapes. Mounted on a scroll, the painting is like a ray of light between heaven and earth. Often, the paintings have decorative silk trim at both ends.

Artist Gary Lau with his completed work.

Those who are artistically inclined and wish to attempt Chinese traditional painting can find supplies **Kee Fung Ng Gallery** at **757 Grant Avenue; Fat Ming Co.,** at **903 Grant,** and **Chew Chong Tai & Co.,** at **905 Grant.**

After you have had a chance to browse in Mr. Lau's art gallery, you may wish to take a break and go directly across the street to **Ping Yuen Bakery** at **650 Jackson,** a bustling pastry and coffee shop/diner. This is probably the only place in Chinatown where you can get a cup of coffee. Take a right turn out of Ping Yuen, head up half a block to **Grant Avenue** and make a right turn. We are headed to the food districts on Grant Avenue and Stockton Street.

CHAPTER 12

Stockton Street is one block west of Grant Avenue and is considered the street where locals shop, mainly for food. However, visitors interested in Chinese cooking should also explore this street in addition to Grant Avenue. The #30 bus, depending on which direction you go, will transport you to Union Square or Fisherman's Wharf. One block west of Stockton Street is Powell, where you may hop on a cable car (look for the brown cable car stop signs).

STOCKTON STREET: WHERE THE FOOD IS

ASIAN SUPERMARKETS

Important stops for the serious Chinese cook are Asian supermarkets and smaller food shops. They have the works: soy and oyster sauces, seasonings, condiments, rice wines, dried noodles, fresh wrappers for won ton, dim sum, egg rolls, and potstickers and other Asian dumplings. Travelers shopping for oils and sauces should avoid breakable glass containers when more durable packaging is available. For instance, an excellent hoisin sauce made by Koon Chun is available in both glass and cans.

Two of the largest Asian supermarkets are the **Canton Market** at **1135 Stockton Street** and **Metro Food** around the corner at **641 Broadway.** Two other important food centers on Stockton are **Wo Soon Produce** at **1210 Stockton** and **May Wah Co.** at **1230 Stockton.** Bins overflow with

Stockton Street is always crowded with shoppers.

fresh produce on display in many of the storefronts. Thousand-year-old eggs and preserved duck eggs, contained in large ceramic pots, are always an eye-catcher. On weekends this street is crowded to the point that it is sometimes uncomfortable, so those who feel uneasy with crowds might consider saving this area for a weekday visit.

Some stops that will capture your attention on both Grant Avenue and Stockton Street include:

CHINESE DELICATESSENS

It is fun—and intriguing—to peep into one of the many Chinese delicatessens which display prepared Chinese foods, some very tempting and others which may appear too exotic and unusual looking to the non-Chinese. Chinese roast pork, whole roast duck, soy sauce duck, and chicken hang above trays of duck and chicken feet; and broccoli beef shares a window front with vegetarian stew, sweet and sour pork, chow mein, fried rice, fermented black bean, stuffed bittermelon, and braised pig intestines or octopus. Whole roast suckling pig with crackling skin hangs in many shops and may be purchased by the pound.

For busy San Franciscans, it is an ideal stop to drop by Chinatown after work to pick up dinner on the way home. This is a simple solution for a meal after a long day at work. The restaurants usually charge by the pint, and prices are considered quite reasonable. If you purchase a duck, chicken, or roast pork, it will be chopped up for you, unless you specify otherwise. Many of the delicatessens are located inside a restaurant, providing a choice of eating in or out.

BAKERIES AND PASTRY SHOPS

For my personal favorites, you will have to detour off Stockton to the **Ping Yuen Bakery and Restaurant** at **650 Jackson Street** and the **Feng Huang** pastry shop at **761 Jackson Street** above Grant Avenue. Ping Yuen is a popular hangout for local men, who make it a daily routine to get together there. In front is a display of traditional and modern interpretations of breads, meat-filled buns, rolls, cakes, and pastries. Take a break in Chinatown to have a rare cup of coffee here (most restaurants serve only tea) and a snack. Mingle with the locals! A bargain rice plate can be enjoyed for a few dollars.

The Lew family operates **Feng Huang.** It is an excellent place to purchase fresh rice noodles for a favorite dish, *chow fun.* Rice noodles are made fresh daily in the crowded back kitchen. Workers are also busy preparing fresh dim sum items, including some of the best Chinese stuffed lotus leaves with sticky rice and rice cakes, and especially steamed barbecued pork or chicken buns. The public is not allowed in the kitchen of the bakeries and delis, but as you make a purchase, you might catch a glimpse of the hard-working staff. One may wonder what the Chinese women are doing while the men relax and gamble at Portsmouth Square. It is not surprising to note that many of them are busy at work in one of over 20 pastry shops and bakeries throughout Chinatown, deftly shaping spoonfuls of minced meat and shrimp into wrappers to form pork

This woman is thinking of all the dumplings that she will make with the filling in the huge bowl to her left.

A steamer full of freshly cooked pork buns.

dumplings and other dim sum specialties. Feng Huang is usually our last stop before lunch, and stopping there is a pleasant way to give our guests an idea of our menu.

OPEN AIR PRODUCE MARKETS

The produce markets add to a fascinating scene on some of the side streets and wide alleys, as well as on Grant Avenue and Stockton Street. It seems as though there are food markets and Chinese restaurants everywhere you look. It's true! As noted earlier, food is very important to us, and since many Chinatown residents own small refrigerators or none at all, they shop daily. It is here that you will find the freshest of Chinese and American vegetables and fruits. The outdoor displays add a great deal of color to the community. Prices are considerably lower than at produce markets outside the area, which is a welcome discovery, and quality is not compromised. Surprisingly, shoplifting is minimal in these markets.

CHINESE- SAUSAGE FACTORY

A little shop near Broadway, **Kwong Jow Sausage Factory** at **1157 Grant Avenue** specializes in cured Chinese sausage, sold by links or pounds. The sausages travel well as they are processed like salami, but must be steam cooked. This shop sells the most popular pork sausage, but I prefer the less fatty version made of lean pork. Other sausages are made of beef or filled with duck liver. The color of the strings attached to the sausage identifies the type. Unusual-looking dried whole duck carcasses are sold for duck broth. Across from the Chinese-sausage counter there is a refrigerated compartment which offers fresh cuts of pork. One of my favorite simple ways to prepare Chinese-sausage is to steam cook it over a rice pot. By the time the rice is cooked, so is the sausage. The rice is flavored by the juice of the sausage.

After walking around Chinatown for a while one becomes hungry, especially when confronted with so many temptations—aromas from the many shops, produce spilling out onto the streets, and restaurants galore. One of the best ways to satisfy hunger during the day is to go for *dim sum.*

Ron the "Pig Man" delivers pigs to many of the restaurants in Chinatown.

CHAPTER 13

What is dim sum? Translated, dim means "point" and sum means "heart": "point to the heart." We choose to describe dim sum as a way of dining that touches one's heart. Others may use descriptions such as "heart's delight," or "touch of the heart." Your dim sum experience can start as early as 8:00 a.m. and last until 3:00 p.m. After an afternoon break, many of the teahouses are transformed into dinner houses with tablecloths and menus boasting complete dinners and banquets. For our guests, this is another glimpse into a traditional aspect of life in Chinatown. Hint: go early. By 1:00 p.m, most of the favorites have been picked over or are long gone.

Dim Sum

A dim sum house can be an exasperating yet exhilarating place in which to dine. For first-timers, it can be tremendously frustrating because generally, there is *no menu*, and the food is presented on carts for you to choose from. If you are unfamiliar with this system, you may regret certain choices, such as braised tripe, pig stomach, or duck feet. Or, the carts may whiz away before you've had time to make your choice! But there's no need to worry about missing a cart. A teahouse visit should be a relaxing experience, so don't rush. Besides, the carts complete their circuits around the dining room, wheel into the kitchen for a refill, and return.

Small stainless-steel and bamboo steamers are piled high on the top of the carts. Unfortunately, they are often covered, so unless you speak Chinese, first attempts at ordering dim sum can be difficult. Smile at the young lady pushing the cart, and look puzzled. Perhaps she will help you out by showing off the food. If you are lucky, she may speak fluent English and will explain the components of the dishes to you. This is a long shot, however, as the carts cannot stay at one table for very long.

Each steamer contains three or four dumplings made of tasty minced pork, shrimp, or beef, steamed buns with chicken or Chinese roast-pork sausage. One cart displays unique treats such as braised and stuffed bell pepper, braised duck and chicken feet, and lotus leaves stuffed with chicken and pork with sticky rice. Another cart whirls by to show off dessert treats, such as custard tarts, sesame balls, Chinese almond pudding, and sweet cakes. It is an incredible sight. I like to sit near the kitchen where the carts come out and make my table the first stop.

Dim sum is a walking cafeteria.

Sharing dim sum with a group of relatives and friends is considered a social event. As the group size increases, you have to order more food! For the total experience, choose a couple of platters of stir-fried *chow mein* or *chow fun* (rice noodles), a platter of fresh steamed Chinese broccoli, and always end the dim sum luncheon with something sweet, like sesame balls or custard tarts.

Michael MacIntosh tastes dim sum for the first time, with the help of Wok Wiz.

In a Teahouse
with the Wok Wiz

By 12:30 p.m., our tour group will have spent two and a half hours learning about the history, culture, people, and food of Chinatown, and we are usually ready for lunch. Our last stop before we go to a teahouse is a visit to a Chinese pastry shop, where we go into the back work area and watch a group of friendly women make Chinese rice noodles from scratch. Another lady fills moistened lotus leaves with glutinous sticky rice, small pieces of roast pork, Chinese pork sausage, a piece of duck-egg yolk, and salted shrimp. With a few twists of her wrists, she turns this into a package and ties it with string. The stuffed lotus leaves are then steamed and ready to be sold. We marvel at the aromatic and palate-teasing displays of rice-based cakes, sweet and salty dumplings, steamed buns, and other delicacies. We're hungry! Off to lunch.

Sharing dim sum with family and friends in a private banquet room at the Harbor Village Restaurant.

At the teahouse, we settle in our seats and relax over cups of hot tea. We sit around reserved tables at a famous Chinese restaurant and soak in the beauty and action in the place. After a quick lesson on using chopsticks and a description of the sauces on the table, our food arrives. We begin with several dim sum dumplings and buns, then complete the luncheon with stir-fried rice noodles with tender beef or chicken and baby greens chow mein. Sometimes we celebrate a birthday or anniversary by presenting the honoree with a dish of chicken feet—the result is hilarious. There is no cultural or traditional reason for this prank. We simply enjoy the laughter. The good sport always tries the chicken feet and sometimes learns to appreciate them. We complete the dim sum luncheon with sweet sesame balls so our group will have sweet and fond memories of our time together.

On Your Own
in a Teahouse

When you enter a teahouse at the height of business, you may be given a number and told to stand back and wait. When your number is called, your table is ready. This may be a little nerve-wracking, but it is a common practice in Chinatown and in other areas as well. At least nowadays, the numbers are called out in English and Chinese. In larger teahouses it is always noisy and carnival-like. If you prefer quieter surroundings, choose a smaller teahouse or restaurant, such as **Honey Court, Pearl City,** or **Yank Sing,** which serves dim sum, regular lunches, and dinners. (See addresses of these spots in the list of Favorite Chinese Restaurants.)

When the carts stop in front of you and your party, take a quick peek and if it looks good to you, start choosing. Be careful not to strain your neck struggling to keep pace with the carts, which seem to come from all directions. Surprisingly, in all my years of dim-summing, I have yet to see a cart crash! This is a walking cafeteria where you sit still and the food comes to you. Sit back and enjoy.

The waitperson keeps track of the number of plates and steamer baskets that land on your table. That is how you get the total bill, plus a set fee for tea. Dim sum is still one of the best bargains in Chinatown.

There is a minimum of 25 offerings at every teahouse. Here is a quick guide to some of the most popular dim sum items in Chinatown:

CHA SIL BOW:
Steamed pork bun. Sometimes they are baked.

CHA SIL OR HA CHEUNG FUN:
Rice noodles with roast pork or shrimp steamed in a roll, served cold or fried.

CHERN GOON:
Spring rolls (or egg rolls).

DON TODD:
Custard egg tart.

FAW OP:
Roast duck.

FUN GOR:
Combination of pork, mushrooms, and bamboo shoots; wrapper of wheat starch.

GEE BOW GAI:
Paper or foil-wrapped chicken.

GHOW NOM:
Beef tripe.

GAI BOW:
Steamed chicken bun.

GAI GUERK:
Braised chicken feet.

GHOW YUK SIL MI:
Steamed beef and Chinese parsley dumpling.

The Harbor Village, at #4 Embarcadero Center, is famous for its dim sum, served in a Hong Kong–style atmosphere.

HAR GOW:
>   Steamed shrimp and bamboo-shoot bonnet; wrapper is made of wheat starch and is translucent when cooked.

HO YOW GAI LON:
>   Chinese broccoli with oyster sauce.

JIN DOOEY:
>   Sesame-seed ball filled with lotus paste.

LEEN YOONG BOW:
>   Sweet lotus bean steamed bun.

LO BOK GO:
>   Turnip cake.

LOT JUI HA:
>   Pan-fried shrimp stuffed in bell-pepper quarters.

NO MI GAI:
>   Lotus leaf stuffed with sticky rice, chicken, pork, and shrimp.

OP GUERK:
>   Braised duck feet.

SEE JUP PAI GWUT:
>   Steamed spareribs.

SEE JUP PI GWUT:
>   Steamed black-bean and garlic spareribs.

SIL MI:
>   Steamed pork dumpling; many with shrimp meat as well. The wrapper is made of thin, fresh flour dough.

WOO TOW GO:
>   Deep-fried mashed taro-root rice cakes with meat stuffing.

In addition to steamed dumplings and buns, try a few entrees that are bound to please your taste buds:

CHOY SUM GUY COW CHOW FUN:
>   Chinese baby greens with chicken chow fun.

GAI LON GHOW YUK CHOW FUN:
>   Chinese broccoli with beef chow fun (rice noodles).

HOUSE SPECIAL CHOW MEIN:

Most often, this chow mein is a platter of pan-fried noodles with a combination of shrimp, chicken, beef, and greens.

JOOK:

Rice congee, served plain or with a variety of toppings, such as thousand-year-old-egg.

POTSTICKERS:

A northern Chinese dumpling with a filling made of ground pork and cabbage, pan-fried on one side, then steamed. Dip into a mixture of rice vinegar, chili oil, and sesame oil.

SING JOW CHOW MI FUN, SINGAPORE NOODLES:

Bean threads or Chinese vermicelli stir-fried with curried shrimp and assortment of meat.

WON TON SOUP:

Dumplings traditionally filled with shrimp, pork, and mushrooms.

CHINESE
COOKING

APPENDIX

In order to effectively prepare a Chinese meal, it is not necessary to have elaborate equipment. In fact, you can probably get away with using equipment from a totally non-Chinese kitchen. The wok and cleaver are the most important, uniquely Asian, type of cooking utensils. For a complete Chinese kitchen, the enthusiastic cook would include the following:

CHINESE KITCHEN COOKING EQUIPMENT

WOK:

A wok is essential for Chinese cooking. The whole idea of wok cooking becomes more exciting and fun. Get into the spirit of stir-frying in your wok! Woks come in sizes ranging from small to large. The ideal wok for a family of 4 to 6 is 14 inches in diameter. For singles and small families, I recommend a 9- or 12-inch wok. This smaller wok can also serve as a supplementary wok, or for deep-frying small amounts of food.

Flat-bottom woks have become popular among cooking enthusiasts and are my favorites for Chinese cooking. The best are made of a heavy-gauge carbon steel, which distributes the heat evenly. An excellent and handy feature on a wok is a set of handles—a long wooden one on one side and a smaller, helper handle on the other side, especially useful for transferring food from the wok to the serving plate. The flat-bottom wok works well on both electric and gas stoves. Some chefs still prefer the traditional, round-bottom woks that require the use of a cooking ring. I use an electric wok occasionally when deep-frying, for soups, steam cooking, and at cooking performances where gas or butane heat is unavailable.

Chinese cooking is very popular, as evidenced by the impressive varieties of woks on the market today. The Peking Pan made famous by Boston chef-restaurateur Joyce Chen in the early 1980s was one of the first woks with a teflon-type coating. Joyce's wok is very well made, not heavy like other woks, and is fun to use. It is marvelous especially for stir-fry dishes that take but a few minutes to cook. With the Peking Pan's success, other fine woks with fluorocarbon coatings are now manufactured by such companies as Meyer and Calphalon. These coated woks require less cooking oil and can be cleaned in a jiffy. Remember to use wooden utensils to prevent scratching the delicate coating.

Woks are highly recommended for the Chinese technique of stir-frying over high heat with great speed. The heat instantly seals in the juices and marinades of meat, poultry, and seafood. Since most of the food is cut into bite-sized pieces, it takes mere minutes for a dish to be cooked. Wok-cooking is energy efficient. In many cases, the preparation, cutting, and chopping time takes longer than the actual cooking.

The basic quick method is to heat up the wok with a small amount of oil, toss in bite-sized pieces of food, stir-fry briefly over high heat (less than a minute for vegetables; 2 or 3 minutes for meats), add a little broth and gravy mixture, and the dish is cooked.

SEASON YOUR WOK:

Before you use a wok, it must be cleaned and seasoned properly. Wash it thoroughly with warm water and soap to remove the oil applied during manufacturing. Dry it inside and out with paper towels, and place on the stove over medium heat. Apply a small amount of cooking oil to a clean paper towel, and rub the inside of the wok to close the pores in the metal. Continue this procedure a few times until the towel stays clean. After each use, wash the wok with a mild soap, and dry well.

If you don't cook Chinese food often, season your wok with a light coat of oil before putting it away. As you use the wok over time, it will gradually darken. The darker the wok, the more you will be recognized as a wok expert.

WOK COVER:

A dome-shaped cover that fits perfectly over the wok. A cover is essential, especially for steaming food. Some stir-frying takes such a short time that a cover is not necessary. If you do not have a wok cover, substitute with any type of cover that will fit the wok.

Typical Chinese cooking utensils: a spun steel wok holds a cleaver, *wok chann* (spatula) and *wok hauk* (scooper).

WOK SPATULA AND SCOOPER:

While not absolutely necessary for Chinese cooking, the wok spatula *(wok chann)*, and the wok scooper *(wok hauk)* do complete the wok set. The handles of both the spatula and scooper are approximately 10 to 12 inches long and are bent a little to conform to the shape of the wok. When food is cooked and ready to be transferred to a serving platter, the spatula is handy to fill the scooper with food and arrange on the plate or bowl.

STEAMER RACK:

Made of metal or bamboo, it fits in the wok and elevates plates of food to be steamed. Bamboo steamers come in tiers and are popular with dim sum cooks. Excellent to use for steaming vegetables and fish, and to reheat food. If you do not have a steamer rack, use a pair of wooden chopsticks: crisscross the sticks inside the wok and fill the wok with water to near but not actually touching the chopsticks.

CLEAVER:

A very important tool. Used to cut, slice, dice, cube, mince, and crush. Use the blade to pound and tenderize meat, and to crush garlic or ginger. All cleavers have wide blades to transfer cut food to a plate or wok. Choose a cleaver as you would a pair of shoes. It should fit your hand comfortably, feel good, and be very sharp. Dull cleavers can be sharpened professionally, with electric knife sharpeners, or the old-fashioned method with a sharpening steel or stone. If you are a serious cook, invest in a good cleaver. I recommend my friend and colleague Martin Yan's *Chinese Knife*.
Note: while your cleaver may appear sturdy and sharp, a special chopper is recommended for cutting through bones. There is a limit to how much the cleaver can handle.

CLAYPOT:

Claypots are among the most ancient of cooking vessels. Modern claypots have a coarse, sandy-textured beige exterior and a dark brown, smoothly glazed interior. They crack easily if not seasoned or cared for properly. Rub the outside bottom surface of a new claypot with cut cloves of garlic until the surface is dark and looks moist. Fill the pot with water; add a pinch of salt; place the pot over low heat and gradually bring the water to a boil for a few minutes; remove the pot from the heat. Let the pot cool, empty the water, dry the pot completely, and it is ready for cooking. Never place an empty claypot on a hot burner. There should always be liquid in it to prevent it from cracking. No matter what I cook in a claypot, I prefer to line the bottom and sides with a few leaves of napa cabbage, mainly to prevent the food from sticking to the pot. I like to use the claypot because it is one of the healthiest and easiest methods of cooking. The combination of food and sauces cooks slowly into a stew, and generally extra oil is not necessary.

SIZZLING PLATTER:

An impressive way to present culinary masterpieces. The sizzling sound always seems to catch everyone's attention. The iron platter rests on a wooden base. Heat the platter on a stove-top burner or in the oven while the stir-friy dish is cooking. Right before serving the food, place the platter on its base on the dining room table, scoop the stir-fry into an attractive gravy boat, and bring to the

The Wok Shop on Grant Avenue has just about everything a cook needs for Chinese cooking, including clay pots.

table. Slowly pour the food from the gravy boat onto the platter. Have a towel on hand, in case of splattering created by the sizzling food.

Chopsticks:

Usually made of bamboo, ivory, or plastic. The bamboo chopsticks are easiest to use, while the others are considered more sanitary. Chopsticks are traditionally not longer than 11 inches. The longer 18-inch chopsticks are used for mixing, stirring, and cooking, especially when deep-frying. To use chopsticks, cup your right hand loosely, and place one stick to rest on the side of your third finger. Hold the other stick between your thumb and forefinger. Now, move the chopsticks so it looks like they're doing leg lifts, up and down. Let the thumb and forefinger do the work. The middle finger should balance the bottom stick.

Draining rack:

Made of stainless steel, the rack fits on one side of the wok and is used to drain oil from deep-fried food. Using the rack allows excess grease to drip back into the wok. The best way to serve deep-fried food is to drain it for a few minutes and then transfer it to a paper-towel–lined plate. This way, the food will be crisp but not greasy.

Wire strainer:

A round strainer made of wire, ranging from 4 to 9 inches or larger in diameter, with a long wooden or bamboo handle. Useful while deep-frying large items in a wok or for picking up sizable amounts of boiled noodles or vegetables.

Typical Chinese Cooking Techniques

Stir-Frying:

The most traditional technique in Chinese cooking. Food is cut into small pieces, seasoned with marinade, and tossed and stirred around in the wok over intensely high heat. High heat is essential to seal in juices and flavors of the meat, poultry, or seafood during the cooking process. Vegetables are usually stir-fried in a small amount of oil for a short time to retain nutrients, hold their bright colors, and maintain a crisp texture.

✧ If food is marinated, be sure to strain it before placing in the wok. Otherwise, the interaction of the liquid and oil will not allow the food to braise correctly, preventing it from stir-frying.

✧ Chicken and seafood are almost done when there is a noticeable color change. Prawns, for instance, will turn from gray to pink, and chicken will be a velvety white.

Quick steps for stir-frying:

1. Heat wok with small amount of oil, swirling to coat sides to prevent food from sticking.
2. Toss in ginger, garlic, or sliced onion.
3. Stir-fry precut food over high heat for a few minutes.
4. Add chicken broth, if called for in recipe, and bring to a boil.
5. Stir in cornstarch mixture to bind the sauce.
6. Drizzle with sesame or hot oil, and top with green onion or parsley.

Steaming:

Steamed food contains less fat and fewer calories than stir-fried, as it usually requires no additional oil. Steaming retains juices, nutrients, and flavors of the food. To steam, place food in a deep Chinese porcelain or glass plate, which in turn rests on a rack in the wok. The rack keeps the plate of food above the boiling-water level as it steam cooks, always covered. Be careful to not use too much water or it will saturate the food, boiling it instead of steaming it. *Always* keep the lid on the wok when steaming. Some popular items to steam are fish, pork patty, and sponge cake. Food can also be reheated by steaming. Bamboo steamers are available in most food specialty stores in varying sizes. They are usually sold in sets of two, with a matching cover. These steamers fit handily in the wok and are great for making dim sum dishes and reheating food.

Pan-frying:

This method utilizes a shallow pan in which food is fried on both sides. Pan-fried noodles for chow mein cook beautifully in a 14-inch fry pan. I prefer using a nonstick fry pan for cooking noodles and potstickers, since it requires less oil.

Claypot cooking:

Food is cooked over low heat in a claypot. Similar
to preparing casseroles or stews, this is an excellent method of cooking for a party. Assemble and
marinate desired ingredients, place in the claypot,
and refrigerate until you are ready to cook on the
stove burner. To avoid cracking, the claypot *must*
be brought back to room temperature before you
put it on any heat. Bring the cooking temperature
up gradually and reduce to allow to cook slowly.
This is an excellent method of cooking, particularly
for a dinner party when many dishes must be
prepared. The claypot will be on its own, simmer-
ing and cooking on the back burner.

Deep-frying:

Two to three cups of oil is the approximate amount
needed to deep-fry food in a 14-inch wok. If you're
not frying a great amount of food, use a smaller
wok and less oil. It is important to test the oil
before starting to fry food. After the oil is heated to
350°–375° F, dip a wooden chopstick in the center
of the wok. If bubbles dance around the chopstick,
the oil is ready. Gently place the food into the hot
wok: do not toss it in or oil can splash and you may
end up with burns. To ensure a clean finish, strain
oil often to get rid of undesired crumbs that settle
in the wok; use a small strainer with a wooden
handle. To keep your distance from the oil while
turning the food, use a long wooden chopstick.
(Chopsticks used for cooking are longer than
chopsticks used for eating.) To prevent fried food
from having a greasy aftertaste, drain it well on a
rack that attaches to the side of the wok (if available) or other type of rack, and then transfer to a
paper-towel–lined serving platter.

A Chinese market in the 1870s.

APPENDIX

Guests on our tours are often amazed at the variety of unusual-looking vegetables on display and wall-to-wall inventory of canned vegetables, regional sauces, seasonings, oils, and dried goods available in Chinatown. Northern California in general has virtually every imaginable produce item available throughout most of the year. We can cook up a storm anytime we want!

For Chinese-food lovers and cooks, no trip to Chinatown is complete without stocking up on some of these ingredients. If you've traveled a long distance to Chinatown, choose sauces and oils that are contained in nonglass jars if possible, or else your suitcase may smell like a take-out container from a Chinese restaurant by the time you get home. Some friendly shop owners will wrap up your purchases for travel or shipment—just give them a big smile.

BASIC CHINESE INGREDIENTS

Stockton Street, parallel to and wider than Grant Avenue, is where locals congregate to shop for all their culinary needs. Stroll along Stockton between Jackson and Broadway to shop for dry goods in the Chinese supermarkets, to marvel at the fresh produce, and to peek at too many fresh and not-so-fresh fish! There are numerous Chinese delicatessens, where roast ducks and pork are on display, as well as Chinese bakeries; however, most of the baked items are Americanized. Between Grant Avenue, Stockton Street, and our many side streets and alleys, you will be able to fill your pantry with all the essentials for grand Chinese meals. Here are a few of my absolute necessities for creating gastronomical memories:

BAMBOO SHOOTS:
Cone-shaped canned bamboo shoots are either
bright yellow or almost white. I prefer the lighter
version. Drain and rinse in cold water. Refrigerate
unused portion in fresh water to cover. Fresh
bamboo shoot is not easy to find, except in select
stores in Chinatown and in Asian specialty stores.

BEAN CAKE, BEAN CURD, TOFU:
Made from a cloudy liquid processed from soybeans
—called soybean milk—this square-shaped soybean
product is very low in calories and high in protein.
Most commonly sold floating in water, four pieces
to a plastic box, it is also available deep-fried,
pressed, or fermented. If possible, purchase fresh,
flavorful tofu in an Asian market. Three textures
are available: soft, usually for soups; medium-soft;
and firm, excellent for stir-frying. Many people do
not like bean cake because of its blandness, but try
a dish called Ma Pou Bean Cake. It's great, made
with minced ground pork and a hot, spicy sauce.
Even if this doesn't turn you on to bean cake, the
gravy is excellent over rice.

BEAN SPROUTS:
From the mung bean, these snow white sprouts
with little yellow tops are best when purchased
fresh. Many stores, including supermarkets, have
bean sprouts delivered daily. Avoid sprouts that are
limp or discoloring, and use as soon as possible—
they do not hold well after a few days in the refrigerator. Approximate size: 2 to 3 inches long. A
delicious addition to any stir-fried noodle dish.

BEAN THREADS, "SAI FUN," CELLOPHANE NOODLES:
A semiclear noodle also known as long rice, trans-
parent noodles, or Chinese vermicelli. Made from
mung bean starch, they are usually sold in 1-pound
–sized net bags, and are divided into 8 skeins of 2
ounces each, held together by pink or red bands.
After pre-soaking in warm water, these noodles
expand to at least twice their original size. Excellent stir-fried as in Singapore Noodles or in soups
and claypot recipes.

Bittermelon, "fu gwa":

Wrinkled green squash, 6 to 8 inches long. True to its name, it's bitter, similar to a strong bell-pepper aftertaste. An extract from the root of the plant, called compound Q, is used in the treatment of AIDS. When I was young, my mother forced me to eat it because she believed it was good for my health. When your mother tells you something is good for you—in Chinese or any language—it usually tastes awful. To balance the bitterness, bittermelon is usually cooked with something spicy, like fermented black beans. If you wish to try it, cut the bittermelon vertically into halves; remove the seeds, then cut into bite-sized slices and blanch in hot water before stir-frying; or cut into rings and stuff with a won ton filling and steam cook.

Black beans, fermented; "dow see":

Black soybeans that have been cooked and salted; they are soft and sometimes seasoned with ginger. A highly popular soybean used mostly in sauces, as with asparagus beef, prawns with lobster sauce, spareribs with black bean sauce, or for steaming with fresh fish. Fermented black beans are usually available in Asian food markets in small plastic bags. I am very fond of a fairly new item on the shelf—fermented black bean hot oil. It's excellent mixed with sesame oil as a sassy dip for potstickers and for cooking steamed fish recipes.

Bok choy, "choy sum":

Nearly everyone knows what bok choy is. It's that vegetable you see floating in your Wonton Soup, or stir-fried with other ingredients. The fibrous Chinese cabbage, with white stems and large green leaves, looks more like chard than ordinary cabbage. *Bok* in Chinese means "white," and *choy* means "vegetable". When I was a little girl, my mother cooked a platter of bok choy almost every night for our dinner. With five children in the family, this was an economical dish—and very tasty, unless you ate it every night. Choy sum is the heart of the bok choy, smaller in size, and gen-

erally more tender and tasty. Choy sum is superior
to bok choy, so it costs a few pennies more per
pound. I didn't eat choy sum until I got my first job.

Proprietor Lincoln Lim of Mow Fung Produce Company.

BROCCOLI, CHINESE; "GAI LON":
President George Bush doesn't like broccoli, so he
probably didn't eat too much of our Chinese broccoli when he was ambassador to China. Too bad for
him, because this vegetable is so delicious. Prepared correctly, Chinese broccoli retains an appeal-
ing green color, and is a little crunchy. Excellent
steamed and drizzled with oyster sauce, or stir-fried
with beef, chicken, or seafood. It is very rich in
calcium and vitamins A and C. Unlike American
broccoli, gai lon is leafier with slender stalks.

BROWN BEAN SAUCE, "MIN SEE JEUNG":
A brown, salty bean paste from the soybean family.
Used traditionally in recipes which include bean
cake, it almost always comes in 12-ounce glass
jars.

CELLOPHANE NOODLES: see **BEAN THREADS.**

CHILI PEPPER, CHILI OIL:

These products add a spicy heat to whatever is cooked. Chili peppers are used whole or minced in stir-frying. For the daring, chili oil is used in the stir-frying stage, or added to seasonings as dip. Be careful not to overuse, as food flavors may be masked by the power of the pepper or oil, and you'll burn your tongue. Chili oil can be made by heating crushed peppers in vegetable oil and cooking at low heat.

CHINESE SAUSAGE, "LOB CHEUNG":

A very familiar ingredient in Chinese cooking. This reddish sausage is usually sold in strings of two, filled with pork, extra-lean pork, beef, or duck liver. The most commonly used lob cheung is made with pork. Great in steamed foods, added to the rice pot, in soups, or minced and added to various fillings for dumplings. Keeps for weeks in the refrigerator or indefinitely in the freezer. This sausage is apparently becoming popular in many cultures. My husband and I were surprised to find a Chinese-sausage factory in Costa Rica.

CLOUDS' EARS, "WUN YEE":

These little wrinkled-up gems are a fungus, a necessary ingredient for Mushu Pork, Hot 'n Sour Soup, and vegetarian dishes. A small handful will blossom into a gigantic mess in a bowl of water. They must be soaked prior to use, and they expand like crazy, so be sure you use a good-sized bowl to accommodate them.

CONGEE, "JOOK":

A common Chinese rice soup or porridge. Similar to oatmeal or Cream of Wheat. (When I lived in Texas and was introduced to grits, they looked just like a small serving of jook to me.) Top the bowl of congee with anything your heart desires: roast duck, minced chicken, thousand-year-old egg, turkey, or raw fish. Jook makes for a very soothing meal whenever you do not feel well, and is an excellent remedy for stomachaches. Try it plain with minced

onions and a drizzle each of low-sodium soy sauce
and sesame oil. There is literally no limit to the
possible combinations.

CORIANDER, "CHINESE PARSLEY":
Also known as cilantro or Mexican parsley, depending on where you live. Coriander has fragile green
leaves and a strong, distinct flavor. Used for garnish or added to some Chinese entrees, and a must
for Chinese Chicken Salad. Use according to taste.

CORNSTARCH:
Essential in the Chinese pantry. Used in almost
every stir-fry recipe that calls for a gravy mixture,
and for marinating foods. A good binding agent for
sauces and for making deep-fry batter. A quick
gravy mixture combines cornstarch with cold water.
No Chinese chef is far from a container of cornstarch while cooking.

EGGS, SALTED DUCK:
Duck eggs preserved in salt water for months. Yolk
hardens and becomes bright orange. Used by some
Chinese chefs in steaming minced meat and ginger,
or in mooncakes. The yolk resembles the moon. An
acquired taste.

EGGS, THOUSAND-YEAR-OLD:
These duck eggs are just preserved for a few
months—not a thousand years—in lime, salt, and
ashes. (The preservation method itself is probably a
thousand years old.) The egg white becomes gelatinous and brown-black, and the egg yolk becomes
green-black. Thousand-year-old eggs are another
special Chinese delicacy. To use, simply remove
shell and slice up. Eat or throw away.

EGGPLANT, ASIAN:
Approximately 8 inches long, these slender, purple-
skinned eggplant are much smaller than American
eggplant. They are delicious stir-fried in a northern-
style spicy sauce (Eggplant with Hunan Sauce).
These eggplant are easy to prepare: simply rinse
and slice diagonally into thin pieces.

FIVE-SPICE POWDER:
A blend of fennel, Szechuan peppercorns, star anise, cinnamon, and cloves. Used to marinate pork and chicken, or in Chinese beef stew, and traditionally in Chinese Chicken Salad. Available in most supermarkets in small bottles or packages, or you can make your own by blending each of the five spices in equal proportions.

FUZZY SQUASH; HAIRY SQUASH; "MO GWA":
Oval-shaped green squash with a fuzzy surface. Remove fuzz with butter knife. Maintains a firm texture while taking on added flavors well. Looks like a tiny wintermelon with a fuzzy surface. Excellent stir-fried with dried shrimp, mushrooms, and bean thread, or in soup recipes. Tastes similar to zucchini.

GARLIC:
Garlic is easy to crush by smacking it with the side of a Chinese cleaver, which pops it out of its skin, making it easier to mince. Garlic is used for flavoring oil for stir-frying, minced for marinating, and used generally in Chinese cooking. Along with Chinese ginger and green onions, it forms the triumvirate of Chinese cooking. To give you an idea of its importance in Chinese cooking, consider the fact that Asians use even more garlic per capita than Greeks or Italians!

GINGER ROOT:
Fresh ginger root is an *absolute must* for many Chinese dishes—minced, sliced, chopped, grated, and used for marinating or general cooking. Has a distinct, spicy flavor. Available in most supermarkets today, and plentiful in Asian markets. Irregular shapes of these knobby roots come in all sizes. If used frequently, may be left out in a dry area, and cut off as needed. Can be peeled and placed in a jar of sherry to cover, and refrigerated. Do not refrigerate ginger without proper procedure because the cold temperature and odors of other foods in the refrigerator will alter the taste of the ginger.

GINGER ROOT, YOUNG:

This is a translucent ginger, sometimes called Hawaiian ginger. Young ginger has a subtler and less-mature taste than the regular ginger root. Young ginger root is easily identifiable because it looks fresh, almost moist, is very pale in color, and is more expensive than the mature ginger.

HOISIN SAUCE:

A dark brown, sweet, and pungent sauce made from soybeans, spices, vinegar, and chili, and, depending on the brand, other ingredients as well. Used commonly in preparing roast pork or Chinese-style barbecued spareribs. My father likes to spread hoisin sauce on lettuce leaves.

HOT MUSTARD:

The best type of hot mustard comes in powder form and is mixed with cold water to a paste before use. Also available premixed in jars. Excellent for dips. I like to mix a small amount of low-sodium soy sauce with the mustard for added flavor.

LEMON GRASS:

Borrowed from the Vietnamese and Thai chefs, lemon grass is becoming a favorite in the Chinese kitchen. Fresh lemon grass can be found in many Asian specialty stores and is usually 2 feet or so in length. It is very aromatic and popular in Lemon-Grass Roast Chicken, cooked with seafood, or used for stuffing chicken. The lemon grass, fairly dried and hard when purchased, is crushed and shredded before cooking. Only the base of the lemon grass, about 6 to 8 inches, is used.

LONG BEANS, CHINESE; MILE-LONG BEANS; "DOW GAWK":

Most of these beans are at least 18 inches long. They resemble green beans, but are milder in taste. There are two varieties: pale or dark green. Both are wondrous stir-fried with meat, poultry, or shellfish, and some fermented black beans, or on their own as a vegetarian plate. Long beans are a close relative of the black-eyed pea, and can grow up to 36 inches long in tropical climates.

MAI FUN, RICE STICKS:
These skinny, translucent dried noodles resemble cellophane noodles. Mai fun is made from rice flour and is traditionally deep-fried and used in Chinese Chicken Salad or as a base garnish for stir-fried dishes. Place just a small handful in the hot oil or it won't cook properly. It takes just a few seconds to transform from grayish stiff shreds to billowing white strands of fried noodles. It's fun to watch them explode in the wok, but be careful not to put in too much at once. Oh, go ahead, drive your friends crazy.

MIN SEE JEUNG: see **BROWN BEAN SAUCE.**

MUSHROOM, DRIED BLACK; "DOONG GOO;" SHIITAKE:
A very popular item in Chinese cooking, mushrooms are sold dried, usually in cellophane packages. They come in many grades. Chinese mushrooms of the highest quality are thick and have pale cracks on the caps. Prices range from $3.00 a pound to over $25.00 a pound.

OIL, CHILI-PEPPER: see **CHILI-PEPPER, CHILI-OIL.**

OIL, PEANUT OR VEGETABLE:
Recommended for Chinese cooking because these oils withstand high temperatures without burning and do not have an "off" smell or taste. The less you use, the better for your diet.

OIL, CHINESE SESAME:
A highly refined fragrant oil obtained from the sesame seed. It is excellent in soups and some stir-fried dishes as a seasoning oil; not to be used as a cooking oil. Sesame oil has a strong, rich flavor and is concentrated, so use sparingly. Stored in a cool place, this oil will last indefinitely.

ORANGE OR TANGERINE PEEL, DRIED:
Dried orange or tangerine peel must be soaked in warm water until softened. Store in airtight container. Used in stir-frying, steaming, and for specialties such as Tea-Smoked Duck. There is much distinction in flavor between the orange and the tangerine peel.

OYSTER SAUCE:

Made from essence of oysters, this sauce imparts an exotic and unique flavor. It does not have a very strong fishy taste and is used in beef and vegetable dishes, and some soups (wonton with oyster beef, for example). There are many varieties and grades of oyster sauce on the market, so prices vary. Read the label and purchase oyster sauce that does *not* contain monosodium glutamate (MSG), the so-called food-enhancing agent which I consider unnecessary in Chinese cooking. Some people experience allergic reactions to MSG, such as headaches, hives, flushed face, and even heart palpitations.

PEPPER, BLACK AND WHITE:

Both are used in Chinese cooking, each with a distinctive flavor. White pepper is preferable in cooking because of its appearance and flavor. If possible, use fresh peppercorns as opposed to ground, as fresh ones have a stronger and more complex flavor.

RICE:

Long-grain rice (Texas and California varieties are popular) is traditionally served with Cantonese and Szechuan food. Jasmine rice has a wonderful aroma and is lighter in texture. Sweet rice is a short-grain rice that is also called sticky, or glutinous, rice. The latter is used in stuffings or desserts.

RICE FLOUR:

A flour milled from long-grain rice, usually sold in 1-pound packages. Used primarily for dim sum pastries and in preparation of Chinese *fun* (rice noodles).

RICE STICKS: see **MAI FUN.**

RICE WINE:

One of the most widely used is Shao-Hsing Wine. It is great for drinking as well as for marinating food. It has a fine aroma and taste. Drink a little, cook a lot! If Chinese rice wine is not available in your hometown, substitute a good quality *dry* sherry.

SAI FUN: see **BEAN THREADS.**

SALT:

I do not use any table salt in my recipes. We do not miss it. In fact, if you leave out salt, you begin to discover a whole world of intriguing food flavors that were masked by the salt. But if you feel it is necessary to add salt to any of the recipes, do so.

SNOW PEAS:

One of the most popular and tasty Chinese vegetables, snow peas are also called Chinese pea pods. They are green, flat pods with a crunchy texture, unless overcooked. When shopping, look for pods that are not longer than 2 1/2 inches, have no marks, and are firm to the touch, not limp. The end must be snipped first and the string pulled off, or the snow pea may be a little tough. Snow peas are easy to grow in your garden, especially in cooler weather or partial shade. Some varieties of snow peas available for home-growing do not need to be strung. They're great to eat when freshly picked.

SOY SAUCE:

Made from fermented and processed soybeans, with salt added. Soy sauce is essential in the Chinese pantry. I prefer to use low-sodium soy sauce. *Black soy* is the type most used for cooking; it has good flavor and a dark color. *Thin* or *light soy* is lighter in appearance and is used as a dip or in stir-frying where little color is desired. Experiment with different brands to find the one you like best.

TOFU: see BEAN CAKE.

WATER CHESTNUTS:

Fresh water chestnuts are the best! The water chestnut is the bulb of a water grass grown in the flooded rice paddies of China. You don't have to go to the Orient for water chestnuts—they are available in most Asian specialty stores. It is easier to find canned water chestnuts in supermarkets. But once you try a fresh water chestnut, you will never forget its sweet taste and crispness. It reminds me of a cross between coconut and jicama. Fresh water chestnuts have a black-brown outer coating, which

must be peeled off. Pick water chestnuts which are
firm, not wrinkled up or with soft spots. They
should be rock hard. Peel the water chestnuts and,
if not used right away, place them in a bowl with
cold water to cover. Use for stir-frying or for snacks.
They're hard to resist.

WHEAT STARCH:

Used commonly for preparing dim sum wrappers
and pastries. Available in 1-pound packages.

WINTERMELON:

Looks like a huge watermelon. It is actually a
vegetable, with a green skin, and white, pulpy flesh
inside. Wintermelons are sold in sections or whole
in Asian supermarkets and are used primarily in
soups. For special occasions, steam the whole
wintermelon: cut part of the top off; remove the
pulp and seeds; fill the cavity with a chicken broth
and other ingredients (e.g., minced Chinese black
mushrooms, shrimp, fresh water chestnuts, or
Chinese parsley); and steam the whole melon.
Serve the soup right out of the wintermelon, from
its self-made tureen. A visual delight.

TIDBITS ABOUT CHINESE FOOD

RICE DISHES:

Order any topping you want over a plate of steamed rice for a complete meal. Try: Broccoli Beef, Curried Shrimp, Barbequed Pork, Barbequed Pork with Scrambled Egg, Roast Duck, Black Bean Sauce Spareribs, and my favorite, Chinese Baby Greens with Fresh Tofu.

DINNER MENU IDEAS:

I'm very fond of fresh vegetables and soy bean products, but will run the gamut of seafood, meat and poultry if on assignment or at a social gathering. I'm also partial to steamed and claypot cooking. Consider variety as you plan a meal.

AT HOME OR DINING OUT:

✧ food should not have a greasy appearance or after-taste

✧ food should **not** contain **MSG** (monosodium glutamate, long considered a food enhancer, but really an unhealthy additive)

✧ food should be fresh

✧ check out the clientele: if a restaurant is dominated by Asians, you're probably in the right place

✧ as in all restaurants, service should be friendly and courteous, and the dinner tab in most Chinese restaurants should be very affordable—even worth fighting over!

RECIPES

THE BASICS

BASIC CHICKEN BROTH

YIELD: **6 CUPS**

> 1 whole chicken carcass or 2 pounds chicken parts
> 1 small knob of fresh Chinese ginger, crushed
> 1 whole yellow onion, quartered
> 2 stalks celery
> 2 green onions, cut to 1" pieces
> 8 cups cold water

To cook: Place the chicken in a large soup pot and add 8 cups cold water to cover. Cook at high heat to near boiling and then immediately lower heat. Add remaining ingredients and simmer at least 3 hours. Drain chicken and vegetables. Cool, refrigerate, and skim off fat from top.

Hint 1: In preparing a dinner party, always have a pot of water on the stove top. As you bone a chicken, put the bones into the pot as well as the tough stems of vegetables, the outer skin of the yellow onion, the core from the cabbage, etc. All the ingredients enhance the flavor of the chicken broth.

Hint 2: A good way to keep chicken broth on hand is to freeze some in ice cube trays. When frozen, transfer 6 or 8 cubes to freezer bags—you will always have homemade chicken broth on hand.

BASIC
VEGETARIAN BROTH

YIELD: **8 CUPS**

8 cups water
1 teaspoon vegetable oil
1 medium yellow onion, cut into eighths
2 cloves minced garlic
3 cups coarsely chopped cabbage
2 cups any type coarsely chopped vegetables,
     including leftovers from the refrigerator
1 medium carrot, cut to 2" pieces
2 green onions, cut to 1" pieces
soy sauce (low-sodium preferred) to taste
sesame oil to taste

To cook: Heat water in soup pot. Bring to near boil. Meanwhile, heat wok with oil, swirling to coat sides. Stir-fry onion and garlic until the onion is translucent. Add all other vegetables and cook for 2 or 3 minutes (don't throw away the skin from the yellow onion or the core of the cabbage—put in the broth). Transfer to soup pot and reduce heat. Cook for at least 2 hours. Add soy sauce and sesame oil to taste. Strain the vegetables and use the broth for cooking vegetarian dishes.

Basic
Won Ton Soup

Servings: 4–6

Have on hand:
  1 pound won ton wrappers
  Large pot with water for cooking won tons
  Large pot with chicken broth for cooked won tons
  Strainer or colander

Filling:
  1/2 pound lean ground pork
  6 medium sized prawns, peeled, deveined, rinsed,
    coarsely chopped
  4 Chinese black mushrooms, soaked in warm water
    for 10 minutes; remove stems, and chop the caps
    coarsely
  4 fresh or canned water chestnuts, minced
  1 stalk green onion, minced
  1 egg
  2 teaspoon soy sauce (low-sodium preferred)
  1/2 teaspoon sesame oil

The soup:
  6 cups chicken broth (low-sodium preferred)
  6 Chinese black mushrooms, soaked in warm water
    for 10 minutes, stems removed, cut to thin pieces,
    add soaking water to broth
  8 prawns, peeled, deveined, rinsed
  1/2 cup cooked and sliced chicken meat
  1 cup Chinese bok choy or baby bok choy,
    cut to 1 1/2" pieces
  1/2 cup fresh or canned sliced water chestnuts
  1 teaspoon soy sauce
  1 green onion, minced
  1/2 teaspoon sesame oil
  hot mustard

Preparation of won tons: Combine filling ingredients, except for the last three items, on a chopping board. Chop and mix well with one or two cleavers. Place mixture into a medium-sized bowl, add the egg, soy sauce, and sesame oil and stir to blend all ingredients.

To assemble: Spoon approximately 1 teaspoon of the filling in center of won ton wrapper. Fold one corner over to form a triangle. Brush left side with a little of the filling. Bring the right side over, twisting slightly, so that the back of the right side meets the front of the left side.

The soup: Heat chicken broth, including the mushroom soaking water. Bring to a near boil. Add black mushrooms, prawns, chicken, bok choy, water chestnuts, or other desired toppings (e.g., snow peas). Reduce heat while won tons cook.

The won tons: Bring 8 cups of water to a boil, and drop in won tons. When water returns to a boil, and won tons begin to float (approximately 4 minutes) drain in a colander and rinse with cold water to prevent sticking. Transfer won tons to soup tureen.

The finale: Pour hot chicken broth and toppings over won tons, arranging the meat or chicken, and vegetables, attractively. Squirt a little sesame oil and garnish with green onions. Have hot mustard and extra soy sauce available.

Note: For deep fried won tons, use 1/4 to 1/2 teaspoon filling. Deep-fry in vegetable oil for just 30 seconds, until the wrapper is golden brown.

BASIC
DEEP-FRY BATTER

1 cup cornstarch
1 cup all purpose flour (may substitute 1/2 cup of the
    flour with prepared baking mix for a lighter batter)
1 cup cold water
1 egg
1 teaspoon baking powder

In a medium sized bowl, mix together above batter ingredients to pancake consistency. Refrigerate for 10 minutes to set. Use for deep-frying seafood, chicken, egg rolls, and vegetables.

■ BASIC THICK RICE CONGEE: "JOOK"

SERVINGS: 6–8

1 cup long-grain rice
1 teaspoon minced ginger
10 cups chicken broth
2 green onions (place one minced in soup pot;
   reserve one minced for topping)
1 turkey thigh, approximately 2 pounds
1 tablespoon soy sauce
1 teaspoon sesame oil

Preparation: Place rice in large 4 quart soup pot and rinse 2 or 3 times in cold water. Bring broth, rice, ginger, and green onion to a boil. Place turkey thigh in the pot and reduce heat; simmer for 2 to 3 hours, stirring occasionally, until rice breaks down completely and soup becomes thick. Remove skin and bones from turkey thigh. Mix in soy sauce, drizzle with sesame oil, and top with minced green onions.

Option 1: Leave out turkey thigh and have toppings of your choice, place in soup pot during the last 20 minutes of cooking: minced roast duck, ground turkey or beef, chicken, raw fish filet, or minced ham.
Option 2: A turkey carcass is perfect for jook. Add it to the soup pot, and remove when the jook is cooked.

Basic Chinese
Rice Noodle: "Fun"

Yield: 5 rolls

Have on hand:
> 14" wok with cover and steam rack;
> filled with 2" of water
> 2 pie pans greased lightly with vegetable oil

Ingredients:
> 1 cup unsifted rice flour or cake flour
> 1 tablespoon wheat starch or cornstarch
> 2 tablespoons vegetable oil
> 1 1/4 cups cold water

In a medium-sized bowl, mix flour and starch together. In another bowl, combine oil and water, and pour it into the flour mixture gradually. Stir to blend until smooth.

Heat wok filled with water. Place steamer rack inside the wok. Ladle 1/4 cup of mixture into lightly greased pie pan. Steam on a rack over high heat, covered, for 5 minutes. Allow to cool, and roll into thirds. Continue this process with the second pan.

Hint 1: May be used for stir-fry chow fun dishes, in soups, or to fill with minced shrimp, meat, and green onions.

Hint 2: Holds well for up to 24 hours at room temperature. Can be frozen for up to a week, but best when fresh.

Basic Steamed Rice

YIELD: APPROXIMATELY 7 CUPS
  2 1/2 cups Texas or California long-grain rice
  4 quart pot with lid

Step 1: Rice should be rinsed repeatedly and thoroughly before cooking. Place the rice in a pot. Cover with cold water and rinse at least three times, constantly changing the water until it is clear. Initially, the water will be quite milky due to the residue left from the milling process.

Step 2: When the rice water is clear, do a final rinse and add fresh cold water to measure 1" above the rice level. Bring the pot of rice to a boil, and when visible water begins to evaporate, cover and lower heat to simmer for approximately 15 minutes. Remove lid and fluff the rice up with chopsticks before serving.

Notes:

1. Texas or California types of long-grain rice are the most common in Chinese restaurants and in homes.

2. Gaining popularity for texture and flavor are Jasmine rice from Thailand and Basmati, from India. Basmati rice requires an extra 1/2 cup of water in Step 2 and 10 additional minutes cooking time.

3. Cooked rice stays warm in the pot for 15-20 minutes. If it looks dry, add a little water and stir.

4. Cooked and cooled rice may be sealed, refrigerated and/or frozen for several days. Excellent for fried rice.

5. Time saver: use a rice cooker.

Basic Sweet and Sour Plum Sauce

Yield: approximately 4 cups

    1 can (15 ounce) crushed pineapple in syrup
    1/2 cup sugar
    3/4 cup white vinegar
    3/4 cup water
    2 tablespoons cornstarch mixed with
       2 tablespoons water
    1 cup plum sauce

To cook: Heat pineapple, sugar, vinegar, and water to boiling. Stir in cornstarch mixture. Cool for 10-15 minutes. Gently stir in plum sauce.

Hint 1: Plum sauce may be purchased readily in Chinatown or in supermarkets that carry Asian food specialties.
Hint 2: May be refrigerated, covered, for several weeks.
Hint 3: Serve at room temperature or cold.

Watercress Soup
Claypot Chicken
Garlic Spinach
Steamed Fish Filets
Steamed Rice

SIMPLE FAMILY DINNER

WATERCRESS SOUP

SERVINGS: 4–5

6 cups chicken broth
1/2 pound chicken meat, skinned, boned, and sliced
4 cups fresh watercress, chopped to 2" pieces
1 egg
1 teaspoon soy sauce (low-sodium preferred)
1/2 teaspoon sesame oil

To cook: Place chicken broth in a soup pot and heat to near boiling; then immediately reduce heat. Add chicken and watercress. Cover and simmer for 5 minutes. Gently stir in egg, and season with soy sauce and sesame oil.

Hint: You may leave out the chicken and substitute 1 cup of sliced bean cake (tofu), or add the bean cake to the soup at the last minute just to heat through.

Claypot
Chicken

Servings: 4

Have on hand:
  2 quart claypot
  cabbage leaves to line claypot
  14" wok

Ingredients:
  1 fryer chicken, approximately 3 pounds. Cut to
    serving pieces; bone in.
  2 tablespoons soy sauce (low-sodium preferred)
  2 cloves minced garlic
  2 slices of fresh ginger, 1" x 2", cut to matchstick size
  8 Chinese black mushrooms, soaked in hot water for
    10 minutes; drain excess water, remove stems,
    leave mushrooms whole
  1/4 teaspoon sugar
  2 tablespoons dry sherry
  2 whole star anise
  1 teaspoon cornstarch
  2 tablespoons vegetable oil
  1 cup chicken broth (low-sodium preferred)

Cornstarch mixture:
  2 teaspoons cornstarch mixed well with 2 teaspoons
    cold water and 1 teaspoon soy sauce

  1 green onion, cut to 1" pieces
  1 teaspoon sesame oil

Preparation: Place chicken pieces in a bowl and add soy sauce, garlic, ginger, mushrooms, sugar, and sherry, and stir together. Break up star anise into smaller pieces and add to bowl. Combine all ingredients and add one teaspoon cornstarch.

To cook: Place wok over high heat until hot. Add vegetable oil, swirling to coat sides. When the oil is hot, brown chicken pieces on all sides. Transfer chicken to a large cabbage-lined claypot. Add chicken broth. Place claypot on range top and raise heat gradually to a boil, stirring gently. Cover and simmer over low heat for 35 minutes. Thicken with cornstarch mixture. Top with green onions and drizzle with sesame oil. Bring claypot to the table to serve.

 GARLIC SPINACH

SERVINGS: 3–4

> 2 bunches fresh spinach
> 1 tablespoon vegetable oil
> 4 or 5 cloves minced garlic
> 1/4 cup chicken broth

Preparation: Clean spinach, trim roots, and cut leaves and stems into 2" pieces. Drain and dry.

To cook: Heat wok with oil. When smoky, stir-fry garlic until golden brown. Immediately add spinach and cook over high heat for 2 minutes. Stir in chicken broth and continue to cook until spinach becomes wilted but is still green and the broth evaporates. Serve immediately.

STEAMED FISH FILETS

SERVINGS: 3–4

Have on hand:
14" wok with steamer rack and cover. Fill wok with water to almost reach the rack, but not touching.

Ingredients:
1 pound fresh fish filets: any whitefish e.g., (filet of sole, flounder, petrale, monkfish)
1 heaping tablespoon fermented Chinese black beans
2 cloves minced garlic
1 tablespoon soy sauce (low-sodium preferred)
1 tablespoon dry sherry
1 teaspoon sesame oil
1 teaspoon sugar
2 teaspoons fresh Chinese ginger, peeled, cut to matchstick slivers
1 whole green onion—gently mash bottom (white part) with side of cleaver to release flavors; cut white part to 1" pieces and mince green part
2 tablespoons vegetable oil
1 teaspoon finely shredded fresh ginger

Preparation: Thoroughly clean the fish. Rinse the black beans; mash with the end of a cleaver. Place beans in a small bowl and combine with garlic, soy sauce, dry sherry, sesame oil, and sugar.

To cook: Bring the water in the wok set up for steaming to a rolling boil. Lay the fish on the steaming plate. Pour the black-bean mixture over the fish. Scatter the ginger and 1" pieces of green onion on top of the fish. Place the fish in the steamer, cover tightly, and steam over medium-high heat for 12 minutes, until the base of the thickest part of the flesh is white.

When the fish is almost cooked, heat 2 tablespoons of vegetable oil in a small pan over high heat and cook the shredded ginger and minced green onion. As soon as the fish is done, transfer it to dining table. Drizzle the oil, ginger, and green onion over the fish. Serve at once.

Vegetarian Hot 'n Sour Soup
Vegetarian Potstickers
Chinese Vegetable Stir-Fry
Stir-Fried Bean Cake (Tofu)
*   with Baby Bok Choy*
Steamed Rice

VEGETARIAN DINNER FOR FOUR

VEGETARIAN HOT 'N SOUR SOUP

SERVINGS: 6

Have on hand:

Soup pot with 6 cups vegetarian broth

6 Chinese black mushrooms, soaked in warm water
    for 10 minutes; squeeze out excess water; remove
    stems and cut caps into matchstick-sized pieces;
    add soaking water to broth

1/8 cup clouds' ears, soaked in warm water for
    10 minutes—cut into smaller pieces

8-10 dried lily stems, soaked in warm water for
    10 minutes; break into small pieces

1/2 cup bamboo shoots, cut into matchstick pieces

1 teaspoon + 2 teaspoons low-sodium soy sauce

Cornstarch mixture:
>2 teaspoons cornstarch mixed well with
>>2 teaspoons cold water

>1 block firm bean cake (tofu), approximately 7 ounces
>>cut into thin strips
>1 tablespoon rice vinegar
>2 eggs, beaten gently
>1 teaspoon sesame oil
>1 teaspoon ground white pepper
>1 tablespoon minced green onion

Preparation: Place broth in a large pot and heat to near-boiling point. Add the mushrooms, clouds' ears, lily stems, and bamboo shoots. Stir in 1 teaspoon soy sauce and bring soup to a gentle boil. When the broth begins to boil, stir in the cornstarch mixture. Add the bean cake, and stir well. Remove pot from the heat. Stir in remaining 2 teaspoons soy sauce, and rice vinegar. Swirl in beaten eggs. Add sesame oil, and season with pepper. Sprinkle with minced green onions.

VEGETARIAN POTSTICKERS

YIELD: 30

Have on hand:
>1 pound potsticker wrappers
>12" teflon pan

Filling:
>2 cups cabbage, cored, chopped fine
>1/2 cup minced bamboo shoots
>8 Chinese black mushrooms, soaked in hot water for
>>10 minutes; remove stems, and mince caps

1 heaping tablespoon minced green onion
1 teaspoon minced fresh ginger
3 cloves minced garlic
1/2 cup minced processed bean cake

1 tablespoon soy sauce (low-sodium preferred)
1 tablespoon dry sherry
1 teaspoon rice wine
1 teaspoon sesame oil
1 teaspoon cornstarch
pinch of white pepper

Set aside:
2 tablespoons vegetable oil
1 cup vegetarian broth

Preparation: Chop all the filling ingredients together and place into a medium-sized bowl and stir to blend. Refrigerate at this point if necessary, until ready to use. Spoon 1 tablespoon of filling into the center of each potsticker wrapper. Fold dough over to make a half-circle, and pleat edges firmly together, approximately 5 pleats. Set each potsticker upright on a platter, so a flat base is formed.

To cook: Heat a teflon-type skillet and add oil. Place the potstickers close to one another around the pan, but not touching. Pour in enough broth to cover the potstickers halfway up. Cover and cook over moderate heat for 8 minutes. After the water evaporates, add another teaspoon of oil to the sides of the pan. Tip the pan to ease the potstickers out of the pan. Remove very carefully with a spatula. Turn each potsticker over, dark side up, and place on a platter to serve.

Serve with: Combination of soy sauce, hot-chili oil, and rice or white vinegar, to suit individual taste.

CHINESE VEGETABLE STIR-FRY

SERVINGS: 4

1 tablespoon vegetable oil
3 thin slices fresh Chinese ginger
3 Chinese black mushrooms, soaked in warm water
    for 10 minutes; squeeze out excess water; remove
    stems; leave caps whole
1 1/2 pounds Chinese greens: your choice, or a mixture
    of :
    bok choy, baby bok choy, snow peas,
    Chinese long beans and/or broccoli
1/2 cup sliced fresh or canned water chestnuts
2/3 cup chicken or vegetarian broth (low-sodium
    preferred)
1 teaspoon soy sauce (low-sodium preferred)

Cornstarch mixture:
1 teaspoon cornstarch mixed well with
    1 teaspoon cold water

sesame oil to taste

To cook: Heat wok with oil, swirling to coat sides. Add ginger and mushrooms. While the wok is still very hot, stir in vegetables in the following order: Chinese long beans, Chinese broccoli, bok choy, baby bok choy, and snow peas. Stir-fry over high heat for a good 3-4 minutes. Add water chestnuts and broth. Add soy sauce and cornstarch mixture and continue to stir-fry until gravy thickens. Drizzle with sesame oil.

STIR-FRIED BEAN CAKE (TOFU) WITH BABY BOK CHOY

SERVINGS: 4

1 tablespoon vegetable oil
1 small yellow onion, thinly sliced
6 bean cakes; slice each bean cake evenly to 6 cubes
1 pound baby bok choy, rinsed well, cut to 1 1/2"
    pieces
1/2 cup chicken broth (low-sodium preferred)
1 teaspoon soy sauce (low-sodium preferred)

Cornstarch mixture:
1 teaspoon cornstarch mixed with
    1 teaspoon cold water

sesame oil to taste
1 whole green onion; crush the white part, and
    cut to 1" pieces

To cook: Heat wok with oil, swirling to coat sides. Stir-fry yellow onion until translucent. While the wok is still very hot, add the bean cake and baby bok choy, stir-frying carefully so as not to break up the bean cake, for approximately 3 minutes until the bok choy is cooked but is still green. Add the chicken broth and soy sauce. Gradually stir in the cornstarch mixture, drizzle with a small amount of sesame oil, and top with green onion.

Wintermelon Soup
Trio of Sea Delights
Stir-Fried Chicken with Lemon Grass
Braised Eggplant in Hot and Spicy Sauce
Tea-Smoked Duck
Steamed Rice

PARTY FOR FOUR

WINTERMELON SOUP

SERVINGS: 6

6 cups rich chicken broth

1 pound section of wintermelon. Remove melon
    rind and seeds, and cut the melon into 1" cubes,
    or leave the rind on, and cut the melon into 1 1/2"
    squares.

6 Chinese black mushrooms, soaked in warm water
    for 10 minutes; squeeze out excess water, remove
    stems, and dice caps

3-4 sliced water chestnuts, fresh or canned

1 teaspoon dry sherry

2 tablespoons minced cooked or smoked ham

1/2 cup minced cooked chicken

1/4 cup uncooked green peas

white pepper to taste

1/2 teaspoon sesame oil

Optional garnish: Sprigs of Chinese parsley.

To cook: Heat broth in soup pot. Add the winter-melon, mushrooms, water chestnuts and dry sherry. Bring to a gentle boil, and stir to mix everything. Lower heat and simmer for 15 minutes. Add ham, chicken, and peas. Cover for another 2-3 minutes. Sprinkle with white pepper and drizzle with sesame oil. Garnish, if desired, with sprigs of Chinese parsley.

Notes: 1/4 cup flaked crabmeat, cocktail shrimp, or minced lean pork can be substituted for, or added to, the above meat items.

Wintermelons are typically available only in Asian food markets, whole or in sections. Whole melons weigh up to 20 pounds and can last for several months after harvesting. Unprotected cut-up pieces will last only a few days in the refrigerator. Wintermelons have thick, dark green waxy skin and white flesh which turns translucent during cooking.

Hint: When wintermelons are not available, you may use fuzzy squash. The fuzz must be scraped off the outer surface before cooking. For soup, cut the squash into thin, 1" lengths.

TRIO OF SEA DELIGHTS

SERVINGS: 3–4

Prepare black bean sauce:
In a small bowl add 2 tablespoons rinsed fermented black beans. Mash the beans with the end of a cleaver. Add the following to the bowl and blend:
   3 cloves minced garlic
   1 teaspoon soy sauce (low-sodium preferred)
   1 teaspoon dry sherry or rice wine

Ingredients:
- 1 tablespoon + 1 teaspoon vegetable oil
- 1 cup of Chinese long beans, cut to 1" pieces
- 1 yellow onion, pieces thinly sliced
- 8 fresh sea or 16 bay scallops
- 8 prawns, peeled and deveined
- 1/2 pound fresh salmon, cut into 1" cubes
- 1 cup chicken broth (low-sodium preferred)

Cornstarch mixture:
- 1 tablespoon cornstarch mixed well with
    - 1 tablespoon cold water

- 2 teaspoons minced green onion

To cook: Heat wok with vegetable oil, swirling to coat all sides. Stir-fry the long beans over high heat for 2 minutes and remove immediately. If necessary, reheat wok with additional teaspoon of oil; otherwise, simply reheat wok and stir-fry yellow onion, scallops, prawns, and fermented black bean sauce for 3-4 minutes. Return long beans to wok and add salmon. Cook for 2-3 more minutes, and add in chicken broth. Gently stir in cornstarch mixture to blend. Top with minced green onion.

STIR-FRIED CHICKEN WITH LEMON GRASS

SERVINGS: 3–4

1 whole chicken breast, skinned, boned, and sliced into thin, 1/8" pieces. Place in medium-sized bowl and marinate for at least 30 minutes.

Marinade:
- 1 teaspoon soy sauce (low-sodium preferred)
- 1 teaspoon dry sherry
- 1 teaspoon cornstarch

Set aside:
> 1 tablespoon vegetable oil
> 1/2 yellow onion, thinly sliced
> 2 cloves minced garlic
> 1/2 teaspoon minced ginger

Combine in small bowl:
> 1 stalk lemon grass—peel back the tough outer
> leaves, crush and mince the bottom third,
> including bulb (approximately 4")
> 1/4 cup chicken broth (low-sodium preferred)
> 1/2 teaspoon sugar
> 1 teaspoon hot-chili paste
> 1 teaspoon soy sauce

Other Ingredient:
> 1/2 cup chicken broth

Cornstarch mixture:
> 1 teaspoon cornstarch mixed with 1 teaspoon cold
> water and 1/2 teaspoon soy sauce

> sesame oil to taste
> 1 teaspoon minced green onion

To cook: Remove chicken from marinade. Heat wok with oil. When smoky, stir-fry the chicken over high heat to seal in marinade. Immediately add the yellow onion, garlic, and ginger, and cook until onion becomes translucent. Stir in combined ingredients and additional chicken broth. Cover and cook over high heat for 3 minutes. Remove cover, and gently stir in cornstarch mixture; adjust consistency if necessary. Drizzle with sesame oil and top with minced green onion.

BRAISED EGGPLANT IN HOT AND SPICY SAUCE

SERVINGS: 3–4

> 1/4 pound minced lean pork. Place in small bowl and mix in:
>> 1 teaspoon soy sauce (low-sodium preferred)
>> 1/2 teaspoon dry sherry

Ingredients:
> 2 tablespoons vegetable oil
> 1/2 yellow onion, thinly sliced
> 2 Asian eggplant, medium-sized, unpeeled, sliced diagonally into thin pieces, 1/4" in width by 1 1/2"-2" long
> 1 teaspoon minced Chinese ginger
> 4 cloves minced garlic
> 2 teaspoons garlic- and- chili sauce
> 1 tablespoon soy sauce (low-sodium preferred)
> 1/3 cup chicken broth (low-sodium preferred)

Cornstarch mixture:
> 2 teaspoons cornstarch mixed well with
>> 2 teaspoons cold water
> 1 teaspoon rice vinegar
> 1/2 teaspoon hot-chili oil

> 1 tablespoon minced green onion
> 1 teaspoon sesame oil

To cook: Heat wok with vegetable oil until smoky. Quickly stir-fry pork until it changes color. Add to the wok: onion, eggplant, ginger, and garlic and stir-fry until eggplant softens, approximately 3 minutes. Add garlic- and-chili-sauce, soy sauce, and broth. Bring to a boil and stir in cornstarch mixture. When the gravy forms, lower heat; add rice vinegar, hot-chili oil, and minced green onion, and drizzle with sesame oil.

TEA-SMOKED DUCK

SERVES: 3–4 AS MAIN COURSE
5–6 AS PART OF A MEAL

4 to 5 pound duck, whole. Wash well, clean out cavity, remove giblets and excess fat. Pat dry. Poke holes all around so the marinade will soak in and excess fat cook out.

To prepare marinade, heat:
    3 cups low-sodium chicken broth with:
    2 pieces of ginger, approximately 2" each, crushed
    3 whole green onions, cut to 1" pieces;
        mash white part
    3-4 whole star anise
    2 tablespoons Szechuan peppercorns
    1 teaspoon minced orange or tangerine peel
        Soak the orange or tangerine peel in warm water for
        5 minutes to soften
    1 cup soy sauce (low sodium preferred)

Boil above ingredients; reduce heat to simmer, add 1 cup soy sauce, and cook for 1 hour. Remove from heat and allow to cool. Rub the duck all over with marinade, including the cavity. Place duck and remaining marinade in a large container and refrigerate overnight.

Smoking ingredients:
    1/2 cup dry oolong tea leaves
    1/2 cup raw long- or short-grain rice
    1/2 cup light or dark brown sugar
    3 pieces of star anise
    2 teaspoons sugar
    6 pieces dried tangerine or orange peel,
        broken into smaller bits

After the duck has marinated overnight, line a 14" wok and cover with heavy aluminum foil. Combine the smoking ingredients and spread evenly in the bottom of the wok. Place duck on a rack, breast side up, in the wok. Smoke for 1 hour. Remove from heat and allow to continue to cook for 15 minutes. Transfer to another baking pan and cook at 400° for 1 hour and 15 minutes, piercing the skin with a fork every 20 minutes.

Many chefs smoke then steam the duck before deep-frying it. Here you can effectively bake the duck with relatively crispy skin, without the additional oil from deep-frying.

Shirley-Fong Torres cooking up a storm.

RECISES

Basic Won Ton Soup
Baked Egg Rolls
"The Good Year Shrimps"
Asparagus Beef
Chinese Broccoli with Oyster Sauce
Lemon Grass Roast Chicken
Prawns Cantonese
Steamed Rice

PARTY FOR A DOZEN PALS

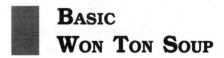

BASIC WON TON SOUP

(See recipe in **THE BASICS** section)

TINA'S FILO TREAT: BAKED EGG ROLLS

YIELD: 8 ROLLS

Have on hand:
Cookie sheet, brushed with sesame oil
Preheat oven to 350°

Filo preparation:
8 pieces of filo dough, 16" x 10", cut into 8" x 5" pieces;
cover with damp towel or plastic wrap
Sesame oil and olive oil in a bowl with basting brush

Ingredients:
- 1 teaspoon vegetable oil
- 2 green onions, including tops, minced
- 2 teaspoons minced ginger
- 2 Chinese black mushrooms, soaked in hot water for 10 minutes, stems removed; mince caps
- 6 large prawns, shelled and deveined, coarsely chopped
- 1/8 head cabbage, shredded
- 1/2 cup bamboo shoots, sliced into thin shreds
- 1/2 cup cooked chicken or turkey meat, shredded
- 1 cup bean sprouts

Seasoning:
- 1 tablespoon soy sauce (low-sodium preferred)
- 1/2 teaspoon sesame oil
- 1 teaspoon cornstarch
- dash of white pepper

Advance preparation: Heat a wok with vegetable oil. When smoky, stir-fry all ingredients in order given above for 3 minutes. Mix in soy sauce, sesame oil, cornstarch and white pepper. Remove to mixing bowl and allow to cool.

Organize work area: Have cookie sheet, bowl of cooled filling, and bowl with oil and basting brush on hand. Also, make room for yourself to work with the filo dough. Place a two-layer sheet of filo dough, 5" x 8" rectangle shape, on a cutting board. Brush lightly with sesame and olive oil mixture. Heap approximately 2 tablespoons of filling 3" from one end of the filo dough. Tuck in sides and roll gently. The edge of the filo should face the bottom of the cookie sheet. Brush lightly again with oil mixture. Cover with damp cloth and proceed to make the remaining rolls.

Bake for 15 minutes at 350°, until lightly brown. Cut into bite-sized pieces.

Suggested dip: hot mustard or sesame oil/soy sauce/ hot-chili oil mixture. Combined to personal taste.

"THE GOOD YEAR SHRIMPS"

This recipe was inspired by my father Richard Fong-Torres. I have adapted it to my tastes, and my brother Ben gave it this cute name, because when they are cooked, the shrimp balls resemble blimps.

YIELD: 16

1/3 pound medium-sized prawns, deveined and cleaned
1/4 cup cooked and minced ham
3-4 Chinese fresh or canned water chestnuts
1/4 cup minced green onions
8 strips of de-fatted bacon (directions below)
16 round toothpicks
Chinese hot mustard (use as dip)
Basic batter for deep-frying (see **THE BASICS** section)
3 cups oil for deep-frying

Seasoning:
1 1/2 teaspoons soy sauce (low-sodium preferred)
1 teaspoon rice wine
2 teaspoons cornstarch
1/2 teaspoon sesame oil
dash of white pepper

To de-fat bacon: Either cook in microwave oven for 3 minutes on HIGH or place on a tray and bake in a regular oven at 350° for 2 minutes (do not allow to brown). Drain well and pat dry. Trim ends to form two halves, approximately 2 1/2" in length.

To prepare: Chop the prawns, ham, and water chestnuts coarsely together. Add green onions and stir until well blended. Place in a medium-sized bowl. Add seasonings and mix together. Shape into little balls; place onto 1/2 slice of bacon; roll up, and secure with a toothpick. Dip into batter, shake off excess batter, and deep-fry over medium heat until golden brown, approximately 4 minutes on each side. Drain well.

Serve with a mixture of soy sauce and hot-mustard dip.

 # ASPARAGUS BEEF

SERVINGS: 2–3

3/4 pound flank, coulotte, or teriyaki steak

Marinade:
1 tablespoon soy sauce (low-sodium preferred)
1 teaspoon minced fresh ginger
2 tablespoons dry sherry
1 teaspoon cornstarch

Ingredients:
2/3 pound fresh asparagus
1 tablespoon fermented black beans, rinsed
2 cloves minced garlic
1 teaspoon soy sauce
1 tablespoon vegetable oil
1 yellow onion, cut in halves, sliced to thin pieces
2/3 cup chicken broth

Cornstarch mixture:
1 tablespoon cornstarch mixed with
1 tablespoon cold water

Advance preparation: Trim fat from beef; slice against the grain into 1 1/2" x 1" pieces. Place in bowl of prepared marinade for 10-15 minutes. Break off tough part of asparagus at the lower stem. Slice diagonally into thin pieces. In a small bowl, combine fermented black beans and garlic. Mash with the end of a cleaver to a paste. Add soy sauce and mix well.

To cook: Heat wok. Add oil, swirling to coat sides. Over high heat, stir-fry the beef, onion, and black-bean sauce. Quickly toss in the asparagus and continue to stir-fry for 1-2 minutes. Add the broth, bring it to a boil, and add the cornstarch mixture, stirring to blend.

Chinese Broccoli with Oyster Sauce

Servings: 3–4

1 pound fresh Chinese broccoli
1 cup chicken broth (low-sodium preferred)
1 cup water
1 tablespoon oyster sauce
1 teaspoon sesame oil

Preparation: Remove tough lower stems of broccoli. Leave whole.

To cook: Fill a medium-sized pot with broth and water and bring to a boil. Add broccoli. Steam cook over high heat, covered, for 3-4 minutes. The broccoli should be bright green in color. Drain broccoli, cut into smaller pieces, usually into thirds. Drizzle with oyster sauce and sesame oil.

Lemon Grass Roast Chicken

One whole fryer, approximately 3 to 3 1/2 pounds
2 whole stalks lemon grass
6 cloves minced garlic
1 small yellow onion, coarsely chopped
2 green onions, crush white part, cut to 2" pieces
soy sauce (low-sodium preferred)

To cook: Heat oven to 350° Rinse chicken and wipe dry. Crush bulb part of the lemon grass and mince. Spread around the chicken, tucking the lemon grass and garlic between the skin and meat. Place the tough outer leaves and woody part of the lemon grass into the cavity of the chicken, along with the yellow and green onion. Pat the chicken with soy sauce. Place on roasting pan and bake for approximately 1 hour, until the chicken is cooked. Carve and serve.

PRAWNS CANTONESE

Fermented black bean sauce:
In a small bowl, place 2 tablespoons fermented black beans, rinsed. Add 2 cloves of fresh garlic, and mash together. Add 1 teaspoon each of low-sodium soy sauce and dry sherry, and mix well.

Ingredients:
1 tablespoon vegetable oil
1/3 pound lean ground pork
1 large yellow onion, cut into chunks
1 pound prawns, shelled, deveined, and rinsed
2 small green bell peppers, cut into chunks
1 cup low-sodium chicken broth
1 raw egg, beaten
Cornstarch mixture:
1 tablespoon cornstarch mixed well with
   1 tablespoon cold water

1 tablespoon minced green onion

To cook: Heat wok with vegetable oil. Over intense heat, stir-fry the pork until it changes color. Add the onion, black bean paste, and prawns, and stir-fry for 2 minutes. Add the bell peppers and broth, while stir-frying. When the broth begins to boil, stir in the cornstarch mixture and mix well for another minute. Slowly swirl in the beaten egg. Top with minced green onion.
Optional: drizzle with hot-chili-pepper oil.

RECIPES

Hand-Shredded Chinese Chicken Salad
Chinese-Style Roast Pork; "Cha Sil"
Chinese Pizza
Happy Birthday Longevity Noodles
Rainbow Fried Rice
Tina's Tiny Almond and Sesame Cookies

BIRTHDAY
CELEBRATION

HAND-SHREDDED CHINESE CHICKEN SALAD

SERVINGS: 4 OR MORE

Have on hand:
> One 12" wok or small fry pan filled with 2 1/2 cups
> vegetable oil for deep-frying
> One 14" wok to assemble the salad

> 1/2 chicken, approximately 1 1/2 pounds

Marinade:
> Marinate chicken for 1 to 2 hours in:
> 1/4 cup soy sauce (low-sodium preferred)
> 1 teaspoon minced Chinese ginger
> 1 teaspoon minced garlic
> 1/8 cup dry sherry

Other ingredients:
  2 ounces rice sticks, "mai fun"
  1 or 2 green onions, cut to 1" pieces
  1 tablespoon rice vinegar
  bottled sesame-oil salad dressing, if available OR: 2
      teaspoons mixed Chinese hot mustard, teaspoon
      sesame oil and 1/2 cup rice vinegar
  1/2 head shredded iceberg lettuce
  1/4 teaspoon five-spice powder
  1/4 cup roasted unsalted peanuts, crushed
  1 tablespoon toasted sesame seeds
  sprigs of Chinese parsley (coriander)

Advance preparation: Bake the chicken on a rack set in a large baking pan for approximately 1 hour at 350°. After the chicken cools, remove the bones and shred the meat by hand or cleaver. Toast sesame seeds in a small fry pan over medium heat, shaking gently, until they are golden brown. Rinse parsley and remove stems.

To cook: Deep-fry the mai fun in first wok. Test the temperature by placing a small piece of mai fun in the hot oil. If it puffs up quickly, the oil is ready. Gradually place small handfuls of the mai fun into the wok. Drain on paper towels. Heat second wok—with *no oil.* Mix the chicken, green onions, and rice vinegar. Turn heat off; add either the mustard and sesame-oil mixture, or prepared sesame-oil salad dressing. Toss in lettuce and five-spice powder. Sprinkle mai fun over the top of salad and toss again. Sprinkle with crushed nuts and sesame seeds. Top with Chinese parsley. Serve extra mai fun and salad dressing on the side.

CHINESE-STYLE ROAST PORK: "CHA SIL"

2 pound boneless pork butt, cut into 8" x 2" x 2" strips

Marinade:
Combine the following in a medium-sized bowl:
1/2 cup hoisin sauce
1/2 cup tomato catsup
1/4 cup dry sherry
1/4 cup soy sauce (low-sodium preferred)
4 cloves minced garlic
1 teaspoon minced green onion
1/4 cup brown sugar
1 tablespoon honey

Preparation: In a large mixing bowl, combine all marinade ingredients and mix well. Allow the pork to marinate from 2 to 4 hours to overnight. Heat oven to 350°. Remove the strips of pork from the marinade (reserve marinade) and place on a rack over a foil-lined roasting pan. Add 1/2 cup of water to the pan. Bake the pork for 30 minutes, basting occasionally with remaining marinade. Turn and baste the other side and cook for another 15-20 minutes. Switch the oven to broil. Broil meat on each side for 2-3 minutes to give it a barbecued-glazed effect, and cool for 10 -15 minutes. Slice into thin pieces.

Note: Use this roast pork for filling in steamed pork buns, chow mein, fried rice, for sandwiches, or to top won ton or noodle soups; or slicd thinly into strips and serve as an appetizer with a little hot mustard. Adding a small amount of water to the baking pan eases the clean-up afterward.
Hint: Excellent with hot-mustard dip

Chinese Pizza

YIELD: 1 PIZZA

Have on hand: pizza tin, pizza brick, or stone oven
preheated to 475°

For basic dough:
- 4 cups all-purpose flour
- 2 teaspoons sugar
- 1 package active dry yeast
- 1 cup lukewarm water
- 2 tablespoons vegetable oil

For the pizza:
- 1 batch of basic dough
- 1/4 cup cornmeal
- 8 ounce can tomato sauce (no salt added)
- 1 pound grated mozzarella cheese
- 1/2 cup minced green onion
- 8 cloves minced garlic

1 cup each of sliced: (mix or match)
- Chinese roast pork ("Cha Sil")
- Cooked chicken breast
- Cooked Chinese sausage ("Lob Cheung")
- Chinese black mushrooms
- Fresh or canned Chinese water chestnuts

The dough:
Thoroughly mix flour and sugar in bowl. Dissolve
yeast in lukewarm water and add to flour mixture. Stir in
oil. Stir until dough forms a ball in the bowl. Place the
dough on lightly floured surface and knead for approximately 5-8 minutes. Place dough in a greased bowl, cover,
and let rise in a warm, draft-free place until doubled in size.
Punch down and knead again. Roll out the dough to form
a circle or rectangle.

The pizza:
    Sprinkle pizza pan or brick with cornmeal. Place dough in pan and spread a thin layer of tomato sauce on top. Sprinkle a layer of cheese and place remaining ingredients on pizza. Top with a thin layer of cheese. Bake for 12-15 minutes and remove when the crust is golden brown.

    Wok Wiz hint: Buy prepared pizza-crust mix.

HAPPY BIRTHDAY LONGEVITY NOODLES

SERVINGS: 4–6

    1/2 chicken breast, boned, skin removed,
        sliced to bite-sized pieces

Marinade for chicken:
    1 teaspoon soy sauce (low-sodium preferred)
    2 teaspoons dry sherry
    1 teaspoon minced ginger
    1/4 teaspoon cornstarch

Ingredients:
    1 pound fresh Chinese extra-thin noodles
    2 tablespoons + 1 tablespoon vegetable oil
    1 yellow onion, thinly sliced
    8 Chinese black mushrooms, soaked in warm water
        for 10 minutes; squeeze out excess water,
        remove stems, leave caps whole
    1 cup Chinese-style roast pork
    8 prawns, peeled and deveined
    1 pound Chinese baby bok choy
    2 cups bean sprouts
    8 snow peas

1 tablespoon oyster sauce
1 cup chicken broth (low-sodium preferred)
Cornstarch mixture:
    2 teaspoons cornstarch mixed well with
      2 teaspoons cold water

    1 tablespoon minced green onion
Optional garnish: Chinese parsley

Advance preparation: Boil noodles in a large pot for 10 seconds only. Rinse with cold water and drain well. Heat a 12" fry pan with 2 tablespoons vegetable oil. Pan-fry noodles for about 5-6 minutes until brown.Flip noodles over and brown other side. Remove to serving platter.

To cook: Heat wok with oil, swirling to coat sides. Over very high heat, sear the chicken for approximately 2 minutes to seal in marinade, and remove. Reheat wok, adding a little more oil if necessary. Stir-fry onion, mushrooms, roast pork, and prawns for 2 minutes until onion becomes translucent and prawns start to turn pink. Add vegetables, oyster sauce, and chicken broth. Keep at roaring heat. Return chicken to wok. Gradually stir in cornstarch mixture. Return noodle cake to wok and break up to mix well. Add green onion and Chinese parsley.

Rainbow
Fried Rice

Servings: 4–6

    2 teaspoons vegetable oil
    1/2 yellow onion, minced
    1/2 cup Chinese roast pork, diced
    1/2 cup cooked ham, diced
    6 prawns, shelled, deveined, minced

4 cups of cold, cooked long-grain rice
1 tablespoon soy sauce (low-sodium preferred)
2 eggs, beaten—**optional:** use egg whites only
1/2 cup frozen green peas
2 cups lettuce, shredded finely
1/4 cup minced green onion
white pepper

To cook: Heat wok with oil, swirling to coat sides. Stir-fry onion, roast pork, ham, and prawns over high heat for 2 minutes. Add rice and soy sauce and cook over high heat for another 2 minutes. Add eggs and mix well, about 1 minute. Add peas and lettuce and continue to stir-fry until the lettuce is cooked. Add additional soy sauce to taste, top with green onion and sprinkle with white pepper.

TINA'S TINY ALMOND AND SESAME COOKIES

YIELD: 6 DOZEN

2 1/2 cups all-purpose flour
3/4 teaspoon baking soda
1 cup shortening
1 cup sugar
1 egg
1 teaspoon almond extract
1 cup crushed roasted almonds
1/2 cup toasted sesame seeds
72 whole roasted almonds
1 egg white

In a large mixing bowl, sift flour and soda together. In a separate bowl, combine shortening and sugar, add egg and almond extract. Mix well and gradually add flour and soda. Stir in the crushed almonds. Form into small balls, approximately 3/4" in diameter. Dip into toasted sesame seeds and flatten to 1/2" thickness. Place a whole almond in the center of each cookie. Baste with egg-white splash. Place cookies on an oiled sheet, 1/2" apart. Bake at 350° for 15-18 minutes or until lightly brown.

DIM SUM PARTY

PORK AND SHRIMP DUMPLINGS: "SIL MI"

YIELD: APPROXIMATELY 24

Have on hand:

    Steamer rack in 14" wok with cover
    1 pound won ton or thin potsticker wrappers

Filling:

    1 pound lean ground pork
    8 prawns, peeled and deveined, minced
    1/2 teaspoon minced fresh ginger
    6 Chinese black mushrooms, soaked in warm water
        for 10 minutes; squeeze out excess water; remove
        stems; mince caps
    6 minced Chinese water chestnuts, canned or fresh
    1/4 cup minced green onion

Seasoning:

    2 teaspoons soy sauce (low-sodium preferred)

1 teaspoon sesame oil
1 teaspoon cornstarch

To prepare: Place all filling ingredients on a large cutting board and chop together to blend. Transfer to medium-sized bowl and add seasonings. Mix well. Cradle a wrapper in the palm of your hand and place a teaspoon of filling in the center. Pinch sides up and shape each one, bringing the wrapper around the filling.

Place dumplings in a cake pan 1/2" apart, and steam over high heat for 12-15 minutes. Serve with hot mustard or combination of chili-pepper oil, sesame oil, and soy sauce.

STEAMED SHRIMP DUMPLINGS: "HAR GOW"

YIELD: 20

Have on hand:
>   Wok, cover, and steamer rack. Water up to 1" from steamer rack. Heat to boiling point.
>   Damp cloth or paper towels

Filling:
>   1/2 pound large prawns, peeled, deveined, chopped coarsely
>   1/2 cup bamboo shoots, minced
>   1/2 teaspoon minced ginger
>   1 teaspoon minced green onion
>   1 teaspoon soy sauce (low-sodium preferred)
>   1 teaspoon dry sherry
>   1/2 teaspoon white pepper
>   1 teaspoon sesame oil
>   1 teaspoon tapioca starch

Dough for wrappers:

    1 cup wheat starch
    1 tablespoon tapioca starch
    3/4 cup boiling water
    1 teaspoon lard or shortening

To prepare filling: On a cutting board, chop the following together to blend: prawns, bamboo shoots, ginger, and green onion. Place in a mixing bowl and add soy sauce, dry sherry, white pepper, and sesame oil. Sprinkle tapioca starch last, stir well, and refrigerate for 20-30 minutes to set.

To prepare wrappers: Sift together wheat and tapioca starches into medium-sized mixing bowl. Add boiling water and begin to knead. Add lard or shortening and continue to knead and blend ingredients. Roll ball into a cylinder, approximately 1" in diameter. Roll into 20 balls, and press down with lightly oiled cleaver to form circles 2 1/2" in diameter.

Hold a wrapper in the palm of your hand and place a heaping teaspoon of filling in center. Fold over and pinch together by making a few small pleats on the top side and pressing into the bottom side of the wrapper. Place on a lightly oiled cake pan, distributing so that they do not touch. Steam over high heat approximately 10 minutes. Excellent served with a mixture of chili oil, sesame oil, and soy sauce.

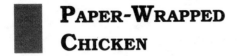

PAPER-WRAPPED CHICKEN

YIELD: 30 PACKETS

1 whole chicken, approximately 3 pounds, boned and cut to 2" x 1" pieces. Place in medium-sized bowl.

Cut 15 sheets of 5" length wax paper. Cut each piece in half to make a total of 30 squares.

Marinade:
In a medium-sized bowl, mix together the following:
- 2 tablespoons hoisin sauce
- 2 teaspoons catsup
- 2 teaspoons brown or white sugar
- 2 tablespoons minced green onion
- 1 tablespoon soy sauce (low-sodium preferred)
- 1 teaspoon sesame oil
- 2 tablespoons dry sherry
- 1 teaspoon cornstarch
- 2 teaspoons crushed toasted almonds or peanuts
- 1 teaspoon minced Chinese parsley
- 1 teaspoon vegetable oil (add to bowl of marinade last to prevent chicken from sticking to paper)

Preparation: Place chicken in bowl with above mixture and marinate for at least 1 hour—the longer the better. Place a piece of chicken and dab some marinade in the center of each wax paper sheet. Fold in half to form a triangle. Fold sides toward the center, and tuck in remaining corner to form an envelope.

To cook: Lightly oil a baking dish. Arrange the chicken packets so they do not touch. Bake at 350° for 6 minutes. Flip and cook another 4-5 minutes.

Hint: Leftovers? Place in microwave for 20 seconds at HIGH to heat through. Do not rebake, as the chicken will be very dry.

SPARERIBS WITH BLACK BEAN SAUCE

SERVINGS: 3–4

1 1/2 pounds pork spareribs, cut Chinese-style to 1" wide strips. (Butchers will usually provide this service free of charge.) Cut to bite-sized pieces.
1 tablespoon vegetable oil
1 yellow onion, diced into 1" pieces

Black-bean sauce:

2 tablespoons fermented black beans; mash with end of cleaver

Add to bowl:

3 cloves minced garlic
1 tablespoon soy sauce (low-sodium preferred)
1 teaspoon dry sherry
1 cup chicken broth (low-sodium preferred)

Cornstarch mixture:

1 tablespoon cornstarch mixed well with
   1 tablespoon cold water

1 green bell pepper, cut to 1" squares, or for extra color appeal, 1/2 red and 1/2 green bell pepper

Preparation: Heat 1 quart of water in a medium-sized pot. Boil the spareribs for 3-4 minutes to get rid of excess fat. Rinse with cold water and set aside.

To cook: Heat wok with oil, swirling to coat sides. Stir-fry the onions and spareribs over high heat for 2-3 minutes. Add the black bean sauce and continue to stir until all the ribs are coated with sauce. Add broth, cover, and simmer for 15-20 minutes over low heat. Bring heat back to a slight boil; stir in cornstarch mixture and add bell peppers. Simmer for another 3-4 minutes, until bell peppers are cooked.

Stir-Fried Tender Beef Chow Fun (rice noodles)

Servings: 4–6

1 tablespoon + 1 teaspoon vegetable oil
Cut 4 strips of rice noodles into 1" x 1 1/2" pieces
   (See **The Basics** section)
1 yellow onion, sliced into halves, then into thin pieces
1" ginger root, peeled and minced

Marinade:

1/2 pound flank or coulotte steak, sliced across the
   grain into thin slices, with:
1 teaspoon soy sauce (low-sodium preferred)
   1 tablespoon rice wine
   1 teaspoon cornstarch

Ingredients:

1 cup bok choy, sliced to thin pieces
1 cup bean sprouts, rinsed
1 tablespoon soy sauce
1 green onion, cut to 1" pieces
white pepper

To cook: Heat wok. Add 1 tablespoon vegetable oil. When oil begins to smoke, stir in the onion, ginger and rice noodles. Stir-fry for 2-3 minutes until it begins to brown, remove. Reheat wok with another teaspoon of oil. Remove beef from marinade; stir-fry over high heat to seal in flavors for 1 minute. Immediately add bok choy and continue to cook—tossing and mixing well for 1 minute. Add bean sprouts, soy sauce, and green onion. Sprinkle with white pepper to taste.

Singapore Noodles

Servings: 4–6

- 1/2 chicken breast
- 1 tablespoon rice wine
- 1 teaspoon + 1 tablespoon soy sauce (low-sodium preferred)
- 1 teaspoon cornstarch
- 4 ounces bean threads (also known as cellophane noodles or "sai fun")
- 1 tablespoon vegetable oil
- 1 small yellow onion, cut in halves, thinly sliced
- 6 dried black mushrooms, soaked in hot water for 10 minutes, drained; remove stems; slice caps into matchstick pieces
- 1/4 cup cocktail shrimp
- 1/2 cup shredded carrot
- 1/4 cup green onion, cut to 1" pieces, + 1 teaspoon minced green onion
- 1 teaspoon hot-pepper oil
- 1 teaspoon curry powder
- 2/3 cup low-sodium chicken broth
- 1 teaspoon Chinese sesame oil

Preparations: Remove skin and bones from chicken. Cut to bite-sized pieces. Place in bowl and add rice wine, 1 teaspoon soy sauce, and cornstarch. Mix well. Remove outer wrapper from bean threads but keep the binding on. Soak in boiling water until the bean threads are rubber-band firm. Using scissors or a sharp cleaver, cut into 3" pieces. Discard binding. Drain well and set aside.

To cook: Heat a wok with oil, swirling to coat sides. Stir-fry the chicken and onion over high heat for 1 minute. Quickly add mushrooms, shrimp, carrot, 1 tablespoon soy sauce, pieces of green onion, hot-pepper oil, and curry powder. Stir in chicken broth; bring to a boil, and return bean threads to wok. Cover and cook over high heat for 2-3 minutes. Add sesame oil. Top with minced green onion.

Lentil Jook (Rice Congee)
Asian-Style Pita Bread
Wok Wiz's Paella

POTLUCK
IDEAS

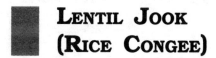

LENTIL JOOK
(RICE CONGEE)

SERVINGS: 6–8

This is a twist on the traditional Chinese rice congee, called jook. My husband, Bernie Carver, from Springfield, Illinois, developed this recipe.

Have on hand:
6 to 8 quart soup pot

1 pound package of lentils
8 cups chicken broth (low-sodium preferred)
1 medium yellow onion, diced
2 ribs of celery, diced
2 carrots, diced
1 cup long-grain rice
4 cups smoked ham, pork chop, or turkey, diced
2 teaspoons black pepper

Advance preparation:

Prepare a pot of boiling water. Turn off heat and place rinsed lentils into pot of water. Allow to stand for 1 hour, then rinse and drain.

To cook:

Add rinsed lentils to soup pot containing chicken broth. Bring to a simmer, add all remaining ingredients, and cook, covered, for 2 hours.

Asian-Style Pita Bread

My father-in-law, Bernard Carver, and I concocted this treat in his home over the 1990 Christmas holidays, in Springfield, Illinois. It was no trouble to find ingredients for this creation in Springfield.

1 package pita bread: 10 halves
1 tablespoon vegetable oil
1 medium yellow onion, thinly sliced
1 heaping teaspoon minced fresh ginger
3 cloves minced garlic
4 cups shredded cabbage
2 cups chopped cauliflower
6 Chinese black mushrooms, soaked in hot water for 10 minutes; remove stems, slice caps into thin slivers
8 ounces cooked Chinese-style roast pork, sliced into thin slivers (optional)
1/2 cup sliced water chestnuts, canned or fresh
1 tablespoon soy sauce (low-sodium preferred)
1 teaspoon sesame oil
1 teaspoon chili oil
1 teaspoon cornstarch
hoisin sauce

To prepare pita bread: Warm up according to directions on package.

To cook: Heat wok with oil. When smoky, add onion, ginger, garlic, cabbage, cauliflower, and mushrooms. Stir-fry over high heat. Stir in roast pork, water chestnuts, and add soy sauce, sesame oil, and chili oil. Continue to stir-fry until cabbage reduces. Remove from heat. Sprinkle in cornstarch and mix well (it should not be watery nor should there be a gravy). Spread pita bread with a small amount of hoisin sauce, fill, and serve.

Note: Be creative. If you are vegetarian, merely leave out the roast pork. Or, choose a favorite seafood or meat for filling, e.g., minced prawns, cocktail shrimp, or leftover turkey.

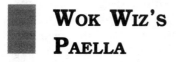

WOK WIZ'S PAELLA

SERVINGS: 6

> 2 1/2 cups long-grain rice
> 2 chicken legs and thighs, chopped into 2" pieces, with bone in

Marinade for chicken:
> 1 tablespoon soy sauce (low-sodium preferred)
> 1/2 teaspoon minced ginger root
> 1 teaspoon dry sherry
> 1 clove minced garlic
> 1 teaspoon cornstarch

Ingredients:
> 1 tablespoon vegetable oil
> 1 medium yellow onion, thinly sliced
> 6 dried black mushrooms, soaked in hot water for 10 minutes; squeeze out excess water, remove stems, leave whole

1/4 pound cooked ham, cut to 1" cubes

2 green onions cut to 1" pieces + 1 tablespoon minced green onion

1/2 teaspoon saffron threads mixed with 1/4 cup heated dry sherry

1/2 cup chicken broth (low-sodium preferred)

1/2 pound fresh halibut, cut to 1" cubes

6 of your favorite type of clams—scrub clean

6 mussels—scrub clean

12 prawns, peeled, deveined, rinsed

1 whole crab, separated and cracked

1/2 cup frozen green peas

1 teaspoon sesame oil

To cook: Place rice in a pot that is large enough to hold 3 times the amount of uncooked rice. Fill the pot with cold water. Stir the rice with your hand; the water will become milky. Washing the rice will remove excess starch and prevent cooked rice from being gummy. Pour the water out of the pot carefully. Repeat until the water runs clear. Fill pot with water to 3/4" above rice level. Cover and place over high heat. When the water boils rapidly, reduce heat to lowest setting.

While the rice is cooking, heat a wok with oil, swirling to coat sides. Stir-fry the onion, chicken, mushrooms, ham, and 1" pieces of green onion for 3-4 minutes (brown the chicken). Place this mixture on top of cooking rice and add saffron-and-wine mixture. Add chicken broth and stir to mix. Place halibut, clams, and mussels on top; cover and cook for 20 minutes. Add prawns and crab, cook 5 minutes. Stir in green peas, minced green onion, and drizzle with sesame oil.

RECIPES

The following is a list of some of my favorite Chinese restaurants in San Francisco. Once in a while, it's a treat to have someone else do the wokking. Here are some places for you to go for good food. Chow fun! Tell them your cousin Shirley sent you. Notice that most of the phone numbers contain the lucky 2's, 3's, 8's and 9's.

FAVORITE CHINESE RESTAURANTS

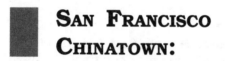

SAN FRANCISCO CHINATOWN:

BOW HON:

850 Grant Avenue; 362-0601. In the heart of Chinatown's most famous street, this tiny cafe specializes in Cantonese stews in clay pots and Asian noodles, stir-fried or in soups. The menu is small but the busy kitchen keeps up with the pace. Inexpensive.

CHEF JIA'S:

925 Kearny Street; 398-1626. This very small cafe has hot and spicy specialties. Go early. Lunch rice plates are under $4.00. Inexpensive.

Harbor Village:

#4 Embarcadero Center; 781-8833. Very popular, excellent Hong Kong–style restaurant in the financial district. Fresh seafood, tops for dim sum. Private banquet room. Medium to expensive.

Honey Court:

760/778 Clay Street; 788-6100. This clean and neat restaurant serves meals off the menu on the street level, and fresh, delicious dim sum on the second floor. Good dim sum and dinners. A shining star in Chinatown. Inexpensive.

Kowloon Vegetarian:

909 Grant Avenue; 362-9888. This popular vegetarian restaurant serves dim sum and a whopping 89 vegetarian dishes. Bean cake and gluten is cleverly used in preparing vegetarian "meat" and "fish" dishes. Inexpensive.

Lucky Creation:

854 Washington Street; 989-0818. Small and crowded Chinese vegetarian hot spot. Casual, bright, and clean. Generous use of fresh green vegetables, beans, whole-grain products, and Cantonese as well as hot and spicy sauces. Friendly and courteous service. Inexpensive.

Pearl City:

641 Jackson; 898-8383. Wide variety of fresh and delicious dim sum available, as well as a good lunch and dinner menu. From the outside, it looks like a small restaurant. Go toward the back and there is a very large dining room for private parties and banquets. Inexpensive.

Royal Hawaii:

835 Pacific; 391-6363. Hong Kong–style teahouse that serves Mongolian Firepot meals in addition to regular and banquet menu. Inexpensive to medium. The owners, originally from Hawaii, also operate Pearl City.

Royal Jade:

675 Jackson; 392-2929. Serves delicious dim sum and complete meals and banquets. A three-level, attractive Cantonese restaurant.

Silver Restaurant:

737 Washington Street; 433-8888. A very informal, casual noodle and jook house. Also popular for lunches and dinner, primarily for Cantonese cuisine. Open 24 hours.

Tommy Toy's Haute Cuisine Chinoise:

655 Montgomery; 397-4888. My restaurant of choice for entertaining VIPs, for quiet lunch meetings, and for romantic dinners. Exceptional Chinese food with a French twist. Excellent service. Extensive wine list. Reasonable lunches. Medium to expensive dinners.

Yank Sing:

427 Battery Street; 362-1640. A very popular dim sum restaurant. On the border of Chinatown in the financial district. Carefully prepared and very tasty dim sum. Many varieties. Medium price range. Open for lunch only.

Outside of San Francisco's Chinatown:

China Moon:
639 Post Street; 775-4789. Located near Union Square, this small cafe offers creative and innovative Chinese dishes, owned by famous chef Barbara Tropp. Medium price range.

Happy Immortal:
4401 Cabrillo Street; 386-7538. A clean, neat, and authentic Cantonese restaurant. Especially busy on weekends as locals flock here for dinner and banquets. Excellent menu. Order in advance their specialty: stuffed boneless chicken. Lunch rice plates are excellent and inexpensive.

Royal Kitchen:
3253 Mission Street; 824-4219. It's worth the ride into the Mission for Harry Lee's saucy clams with black-bean sauce and homemade potstickers. Very casual and popular neighborhood restaurant. This may sound strange, but one of my favorite items to order is their pesto pizza, reeking of freshly minced garlic. Inexpensive.

BIBLIOGRAPHY

RECOMMENDED BOOKS TO READ:

Chinese Historical Society of America.
Chinese America: History and Perspective. Brisbane, California: Chinese Historical Society of America, 1990.

Chinn, Thomas.
A History of the Chinese in California. San Francisco: Chinese Historical Society of America, 1969.

Bridging the Pacific. San Francisco: Chinese Historical Society of America, 1989.

Chow, Kit, and Ione Kramer.
All the Tea in China. San Francisco: China Books & Periodicals, 1990.

Cole, Tom.
A Short History of San Francisco. San Francisco: Don't Call It Frisco Press, 1988.

Delehanty, Randolph.
San Francisco: The Ultimate Guide. San Francisco: Chronicle Books, 1989.

Dickson, Samuel.
Tales of San Francisco. Stanford: Stanford University Press, 1947.

Dobie, Charles Calwell.
San Francisco's Chinatown. New York: D. Appleton-Century Company, 1936.

Gordon, Mark.
Once Upon A City. San Francisco: Don't Call It Frisco Press, 1988.

Long, Jean.
How to Paint the Chinese Way. New York: Blandford Press, 1979.

Martin, Mildred Crowl.
Chinatown's Angry Angel. Palo Alto: Pacific Books, 1977.

Schoenman, Theodore.
The Father of California Wine: Agoston Haraszthy. Santa Barbara: Capra Books, 1979.

Stalberg, Roberta Helmer, and Ruth Nesi.
China's Crafts. New York: Eurasia Press, 1980.

Takaki, Ronald.
Strangers from a Different Shore. Boston: Little, Brown and Company, 1989.

Teeguarden, Ron.
Chinese Tonic Herbs. New York: Japan Publications, 1985.

Walters, Derek.
Feng Shui. New York: Simon & Schuster, 1988.

RECOMMENDED COOKBOOKS:

Burum, Linda.
Asian Pasta. Berkeley: Aris Books, 1985.

Chan, Henry, and Yukiko and Bob Haydock.
Classic Deem Sum. New York: Holt, Rinehart and Winston, 1985.

Chu, Lawrence.
Distinctive Cuisine of China. Harper & Row, 1984.

Chung, Henry.
Henry Chung's Hunan Style Chinese Cookbook. Harmony Books, 1978.

Cost, Bruce.
Bruce Cost's Asian Ingredients. New York: William Morrow and Company, 1988.

Kan, Johnny and Charles Leong.
Eight Immortal Flavors. San Francisco: A Johnny Kan Book, 1963.

Kan, Lilah.
Introducing Chinese Casserole Cookery. New York: Workman Publishing, 1978.

Simonds, Nina.
Chinese Seasons. Boston: Houghton Mifflin Company, 1986.

Tropp, Barbara.
The Modern Art of Chinese Cooking. New York: William Morrow, 1982.

Yin-Fei Lo, Eileen.
The Chinese Banquet Cookbook. New York: Crown Publishers, 1985.

Yee, Rhoda.
Dim Sum. San Francisco: Taylor & Ng, 1977.

Yan, Martin.
Everybody's Wokking. New York: Doubleday, 1991.
A Wok for All Seasons. New York: Doubleday, 1988.

For more information about walking tours and cooking programs contact:

Wok Wiz™

CHINATOWN TOURS
& COOKING COMPANY

✧

P.O. Box 1583
Pacifica, CA 94044

✧

PHONE: (415) 355-9657
FAX: (415) 355-5928